Curling

The History,

The Players,

The Game

Curling

The History,
The Players,
The Game

W A R R E N   H A N S E N

Foreword by Kevin Martin

KEY PORTER BOOKS

Photo Credits:
Michael Burns: 17, 27, 33, 34, 38, 39 (right), 40, 41, 43 (right), 50, 51, 52, 53, 58, 60, 65, 67, 71, 76, 79, 83, 85, 87, 93, 96, 107, 108, 109 (figures 5.3, 5.4), 110, 115, 131, 137 (figures 5.54, 5.55), 141 (bottom), 143; Inter Nationes e. V.: 21; Erwin A. Sautter: 22, 44, 45; Athlete Information Bureau/ Canadian Olympic Association: 46, 47; Morris Studios: 61; Woodland Studio: 63; Pat Humphreys/ *Calgary Herald*: 66; Mike Ridewood: 141 (top); Bild: 142

Canadian Cataloguing in Publication Data

Hansen, Warren
    Curling: the history, the players, the game

ISBN 1-55263-083-8

1. Curling — History. I. Title

GV845.H356 1999   796.964   C99-931507-2

THE CANADA COUNCIL | LE CONSEIL DES ARTS
FOR THE ARTS | DU CANADA
SINCE 1957 | DEPUIS 1957

The publisher gratefully acknowledges the support of the Canada Council for the Arts and the Ontario Arts Council for its publishing program.

Canadä

We acknowledge the financial support of the Government of Canada through the Book Publishing Industry Development Program (BPIDP) for our publishing activities.

Key Porter Books Limited
70 The Esplanade
Toronto, Ontario
Canada M5E 1R2

www.keyporter.com

Design: Peter Maher
Electronic formatting: Heidi Palfrey

Printed and bound in Spain by Bookprint, S.L.,Barcelona

99 00 01 02 03 6 5 4 3 2 1

*To the memory of Bill Good Sr., Hector Gervais, Ray Kingsmith, and Herb Millham.
All four of these gentlemen made an outstanding contribution
to the game of curling during their lives, and each in his own way
had a dramatic impact on my involvement with the sport.*

Contents

Acknowledgments

For many years I have wanted to capture on paper some of the knowledge gained from my forty-plus years in curling as a player, instructor, coach, equipment entrepreneur, media member, and event manager.

It all became a reality when Anna Porter contacted me in the fall of 1998 and asked if I would be interested in writing a book about curling. For the original idea and the confidence in having me do the job, I would like to thank Anna. Also, a special thanks to my editor at Key Porter, Barbara Berson, for her insight into the type of content this book really had to have to make it attractive to curlers and non-curlers alike.

A very special thank-you to Dave Komosky, who spent hours editing and rewriting player biographies and the championship section. Without your help, Dave, it would never have all come together.

Larry Wood has worked with me for years producing the Extra End Annual and the various programs for the Season of Champions events. Thanks also to Larry for his work on the player biographies and all of the many things he has taught me about writing over the years.

To my working colleagues at the Canadian Curling Association, Gerry Peckham and Neil Houston, thank you as well for all your help. I consulted both Neil and Gerry on a number of the technical aspects of the book. Neil was kind enough to make himself available as a model for many of the photographs in the delivery section.

Michael Burns, Sr. and Jr., have been the photographers of choice for curling worldwide for over thirty years. The majority of the images in this book have been produced by Michael Burns Photography and I would like to thank Michael Burns Jr. for his help in shooting and producing the photos.

WARREN HANSEN
JUNE 1999

Foreword

The sport of curling has experienced an explosion in numbers and popularity during the 1990s. In the early part of the decade, curling had high interest in terms of participation, but was struggling to make its mark in the spectator-sport marketplace. In 1994, the Canadian Curling Association approved the three-rock Free Guard Zone (FGZ) rule, which led to a new, aggressive, high-scoring style of curling that was an instant success, with fans and curlers alike.

Curling made its first appearance as a medal sport in the Winter Olympics in 1988, after a fifteen-year struggle to gain full Olympic status. By the latter part of the decade, all of curling's major championships were drawing record crowds, and had television ratings that were the envy of every amateur sport in Canada. In addition, participation in junior curling, and all aspects of grass-roots participation, have risen notably since 1990. Things have also improved dramatically for the competitive curlers, and the introduction of the World Curling Tour (WCT) has increased the purses for competitors in the fall of each year.

Curling's largest event is still the Brier, a competition that has been a pillar of Canadian sport culture since 1927. It is only in the past few years, however, that the Brier has emerged as a sport event that is comparable to the Stanley Cup and the Grey Cup.

The change in the prominence of the Brier was largely due to a decision in 1994, made by the Canadian Curling Association (CCA): Warren Hansen (author of this book) persuaded the CCA to move the Brier from medium-sized arenas (4,000–6,000 seats) to larger venues. The small-venue Briers were almost always sold out and, in the majority of cases, very successful. It is difficult to convince anyone to gamble by changing something that is already successful. However, Warren was so confident that curling could attract 15,000-plus crowds in major-market coliseums that he took that chance. And what a risk, with a move to the 18,000-seat Calgary Olympic Saddledome. Many curlers and fans doubted curling's ability to attract such a crowd in a major competitive market, but Hansen was able to forge ahead, despite the doubters. The final outcome, with a total attendance of 223,000-plus, confirmed that his optimism had been warranted.

Our team was fortunate enough to represent Alberta at the 1997 Brier. Without question, it was the most exciting sporting experience of my life. We played the final game against Manitoba's Vic Peters before nearly 18,000 cheering people. It sent chills down my spine. So I give Warren full credit for having the vision to send the Brier in a new and very exciting direction.

Like many of Canada's curlers, I remember Warren was a championship curler in the late 1960s and 1970s. He was part of the legendary Hec Gervais team that captured the Brier title in 1974. A number of years later, I had the opportunity to be associated with him through the various Canadian and world championships I competed in. Our team traveled and was closely associated with Warren in the leadup to, and during, the 1992 Winter Olympic Games at Albertville, France. During my years of competitive curling, the name Warren Hansen has been synonymous with the sport and the CCA.

Someone who undertakes to write a book about a sport must be knowledgeable about all facets of the game. Warren has competed at the top level, including the Brier, the world championship, and the bonspiel circuit. He has been an event manager, a builder and promoter of curling, and a friend of the curlers. I can't think of anyone better qualified to write *Curling: The History, The Players, The Game*. I hope you enjoy this book as much as I have.

KEVIN MARTIN
JULY 1999

Introduction

I was about ten years old when I first became aware of curling, and I instantly fell in love with the game. I grew up in the small farming community of Namao, about 10 miles (16 km) north of Edmonton, Alberta. My parents were middle-aged when friends first invited them to participate in the game of curling. There were no curling facilities in the area, so they took a half-hour car ride to the Thistle Curling Club in Edmonton to play. Many evenings I went with them and sat behind the glass to watch the action. I could hardly wait to grow up and get a chance to play this intriguing game.

When I turned thirteen, it seemed my dream would come true. The Canadian Forces Base not far from my home had built a curling facility and was making it available to area residents. The physical education staff at Namao School arranged with the club for a group of students to play once a week after school. I was ecstatic. I was finally going to have my chance to participate . . . or so I thought. Alas, the school league was scheduled for Tuesday after school, which happened to coincide with my weekly piano lesson in Edmonton. My mother was not about to let me pass on the piano lesson in favor of curling. My first opportunity to throw a curling rock the length of the sheet was snatched away.

I barely endured the winter, listening to my schoolmates discuss the fun they were having in the weekly league. But all was not lost. Our school was going to hold a spring bonspiel at the air base, and I had my name on the players' list minutes after it was posted. Although I had never curled a game, I believed the hours of watching from behind the glass were worth something. I registered as a second.

It was glorious fun. Unhindered by inexperience, I took to the game with unabashed glee. The first few shots weren't pretty, but I was able to get them to the other end. Sweeping was a little tougher. I barely managed to get from end to end without kicking the stone. Somehow, we placed fourth in the second event, and I had won my first curling prize—a green pen-and-pencil set. I was hooked. Over the next few winters, I devoted as much time as possible to the game.

WARREN HANSEN
CANADIAN CHAMPION

In December 1959, a poster advertising a high-school Christmas bonspiel at the Balmoral Club in Edmonton caught my eye. I managed to convince three of my curling buddies to join me, including the school's most successful skip, Norman Carruthers. We were starry-eyed, to be sure, playing against the city kids, and lost our opening game. But things started to come together and, before we knew it, we had won five consecutive games and were the second-event champions. By the end of the bonspiel, we four kids from the country showed we could play.

The sky was now the limit. I remember seeing the big, bold Pepsi Cola poster advertising the Canadian junior final in Noranda, Quebec. I imagined our team making it all the way. We entered the high-school playdowns in mid-January and traveled about 50 miles (80 km) north to the town of Westlock to play in a twelve-team, rural-zone playdown. The magic was still there. We swept the zone championship in four straight games and earned the right to play in the Northern Alberta championship in Edmonton. But it was over for us in two straight games. Tom Kroeger, a sixteen-year-old from Settle, won the northern championship and went on to win the provincial and Canadian championships as well. He immediately became my curling idol.

In the fall of 1961, I registered at Alberta College in Edmonton to complete Grade 12. I signed up for the curling league and, to my great surprise, discovered Kroeger was also attending the college. Somehow, I convinced him to take me on as his second, and our team was immediately recognized as the one to beat in Northern Alberta.

We started the zone playdowns in January and waltzed through with little resistance. Next up, the Northern Alberta championship, which we saw as only a formality. But that's when I learned my first great curling lesson: There is never a sure thing. We were upset by Brian Taylor, who beat us in two straight games in the final.

I made my breakthrough in men's curling over the next half-dozen years, taking my share of lumps. In 1962, the same year we lost the Northern juniors, another team from Northern Alberta, skipped by big Hector Gervais, came within an eyelash of winning a second consecutive Brier in Kitchener, eventually falling in a playoff to the great Ernie Richardson. Gervais's third was Ron Anton, only a couple of years older than me, an outstanding shooter with a unique way of delivering: he would turn his sliding foot sideways to provide nearly perfect balance. I was intrigued with Anton and his style, and changed from the standard toe-tuck delivery to the Anton-style balanced slide. It wasn't an easy transition, but I eventually mastered it.

I reunited with one of my mates from the Kroeger schoolboy team, Wayne McElroy, in 1967. McElroy skipped and I played second on a team that managed to win an Edmonton zone position. I moved up to third the following year, and Bob Esdale joined us to play second. Esdale had played second for Gervais through 1965 and 1966, and was Anton's good friend. This time we went through the A side of the city playdowns, defeating

Gervais and Anton in the A final. We were off to the Northern Alberta championship, where we won the A side of the double-knockout competition. But once again disaster struck. This time it was Dr. Bill Mitchell who came up the B side of the playoff to knock us off in two straight games.

I briefly gave skipping a whirl in 1969 but soon abandoned the idea. It wasn't for me. So, in 1970, I joined Anton's team, which included Esdale at second. I was now playing third for a player I had idolized as a junior. The next two seasons were good ones for our team, and we finished close to the top in Western Canada on the bonspiel circuit. But we couldn't get out of the Edmonton playdowns, so it was back to the drawing board in 1972.

Many things in life happen by chance. That's how I met Jim Pettapiece in December 1971. Anton, a teacher, was a last-minute scratch in an Edmonton carspiel because of job demands. Pettapiece, just coming off a second world championship with Winnipeg's Don Duguid, was in Edmonton taping the annual "Keen Ice" show with CBC television. Pettapiece had not planned to play in the carspiel, but organizer Wally Ursluliak convinced him to stay and play for Anton. Pettapiece and I had never met, and did not do well in the bonspiel, but we did set up what would prove to be an interesting relationship.

Pettapiece, through his involvement with the world curling championships, sponsored then by Air Canada and known as the "Silver Broom," had developed a solid relationship with a number of people at the top of the corporate ladder at Air Canada. We talked about setting up an international curling school that Air Canada could sponsor. Pettapiece did much of the legwork, and the Silver Broom Curling School made its appearance in October 1972.

I resigned my job in the telecommunications industry in 1972 to work full-time in curling. At the time it looked like a crazy idea. Then, the bubble burst, and the Silver Broom Curling School was soon floundering in a sea of red ink. But we pressed on, borrowing more money and setting plans to return in the fall of 1973. The Silver Broom School moved coast-to-coast across Canada, and into the northeastern United States, the following year, and had a fair degree of success.

Meanwhile, on the competitive scene, Anton and I decided that, after three years of failing to win a berth in the City of Edmonton Brier playdowns, it was time for a change. The curling school business and my existing curling equipment enterprises were also placing more demands on my time. Anton suggested getting Gervais to skip. I wasn't so sure. Hector was a great player, but he had struggled from time to time in the late 1960s. Anton was convincing, though, and a new team was formed for the 1972–73 season. Eventually, he would lead us to a Brier title and a trip to the world championship.

The Silver Broom Curling School was percolating right along by the winter of 1974 and, although two other professional teaching operations were in existence, we had managed to grab a large share of the market.

By now we had three full-time and a dozen part-time instructors. The Canadian Curling Association (CCA) had stayed clear of the teaching business up until then, but a number of delegates felt the association needed to get involved. The CCA budgeted $3,000 in 1974 to establish a presence in the area of instruction the following year.

I was at the Brier as a member of the Alberta team in 1974 and was unaware of what was happening in the boardroom. However, my good friend Ray Kingsmith, who was there as an Alberta delegate, informed me of the CCA plans to get into the instruction business. Kingsmith set up a meeting with me and the newly elected third vice-president, Herb Millham, to work out the details. It was a historic meeting because it paved the way for the Curl Canada development program, and the eventual establishment of the Curl Canada and the CCA offices at the National Sport Centre in Ottawa.

I signed my first contract with the CCA in 1974 and was handed the responsibility for establishing a teaching standard for curling in Canada. The CCA administration at that time was small potatoes and directed out of the basement office of a part-time secretary-treasurer in Winnipeg. The books of the Canadian Ladies Curling Association traveled from one president's kitchen table to the next. I was the first person the CCA paid to perform a task directly related to the sport of curling.

The program made giant strides in the late 1970s and, by 1980, the Curl Canada system was working well across Canada. Meanwhile, I had further developed my interests in the curling equipment business, and the Silver Broom Curling School was still prospering. I had also branched out to the media side of curling, doing radio reports for a number of stations from the major championships, and writing on technical issues. When I accepted the challenge from the CCA to establish the Curl Canada training system, I knew it would eventually be the end of the Silver Broom school. The plug was pulled on the school in the spring of 1979.

I moved further into the curling equipment business and took on a new career path with the CCA that was more focused on public relations, media, and marketing. I moved from Alberta to Vancouver in 1975 to curl, and joined Jim Armstrong at third. We played together from 1976 to 1980, when I finally decided that my many diversified interests in curling were making it impossible to be a dedicated player. I quit throwing rocks in anger but still maintained a close affiliation with the technical aspects of the sport. I was the CCA-appointed team leader for the men's teams, participating at the world championship from 1980 to 1991, and I continue to be a student of the game.

Through the 1980s and into the 1990s, my role with the Canadian Curling Association went through a number of changes that have coincided with the growth of curling. Today, I'm responsible for the management of the CCA major championships and the association's media relations. In September 1999, I celebrated my twenty-fifth year as a contractee of the CCA. The sport has been a dominant force throughout most of my adult

The 1974 Brier champions: from the left, Hector Gervais, Ron Anton, Warren Hansen, and Darrell Sutton.

years, and I'm the first person who actually turned my passion for curling into a business and a livelihood.

I have participated in numerous sporting activities, both recreationally and competitively, during my life, so I think I'm safe in saying that curling is one of the most difficult skills to master. While it is relatively easy and inexpensive to play at a recreational level, it offers the ultimate challenge to the elite player. No one has ever won a national or international crown in curling without hundreds of dedicated hours in practice and training.

I have endeavored in this book to offer you some of the knowledge I have gained about curling over the past forty years. This book has something for everyone, whether a seasoned veteran of the sport, an enthusiastic newcomer, or simply an armchair skip who enjoys watching the dozens of hours of coverage provided annually across Canada on TSN, CBC, and Sportsnet. Curling is a unique sport and there has been far too little written about it over the past fifty years. I hope this book helps to fill some of that void.

Curling's History

What do you know about curling—I mean *really* know? Many people curl all their lives without knowing anything more than the rules and moves of the game.

That's too bad, because there is a lot to be gained by understanding any subject, including the wonderful game of curling. Beyond the joy that learning things for their own sake brings, there is a certain delightful smugness in knowing something about a subject that somebody else doesn't. It raises you to a new level when you become knowledgeable about things many others take for granted.

Let's say you casually mention to a friend over post-game refreshments that the name of the sport originally had nothing to do with the curling motion of the stones on their way down the ice (that's true). "Really?" your friend says. "I never knew that." See? People begin to look at you in a different light.

It's one thing to play a game, but it's another to know something about it—its lore, its famous figures, its historical development. Certainly it was fun for me to sift through curling's past. But, at the same time, the search led to some startling discoveries, as you will see.

Writers often poke fun at a sport's early beginnings. Curling has not been spared. Columnist Rob Tychkowski of the *Edmonton Sun* wrote about the origins of the game in a tongue-in-cheek column during the 1999 Labatt Brier:

> Curling first originated in 610 B.C. with cavemen rolling large stones at a sleeping, flesh-eating dinosaur. Four guys, one on each side, standing 50 feet from a snoozing T-Rex. The object was to take turns rolling rocks as close as possible without actually waking the vicious carnivore and being eaten alive. They called it the roaring game. Roll it too close and, heaven forbid, hit the dinosaur, and it was: "Ugh! Poor Thag."
>
> This is also where the expression "Hurry! Hurry!" first originated. It was the last thing guys like Thag would hear while running for their lives.

Bob Vanstone, a curling writer with the *Regina Leader-Post*, also had some fun with the game's past: "The world's first documented curling injury—the hernia—is sustained by a Scottish soldier who attempts to lift a 120-pound curling stone. The soldier pleads for assistance from a doctor but settles for an inturn."

Alas, curling historians are denied such drama: there is no evidence of loss of life or blood-curdling screams associated with the game's origins.

So when, and where, did curling actually begin? Who invented it, and why was it called curling? We can be sure of one thing: there is no Abner Doubleday or John Naismith in curling's past. Doubleday is credited for inventing baseball, and Canada's Naismith nailed up peach baskets and created basketball in a YMCA gym, but curling has no such founder. The game merely evolved, over time, from rather simple beginnings.

SCOTLAND: THE GAME IS BORN

Ask curlers anywhere to name the birthplace of curling and they will answer, "Why, Scotland, of course." And they're right. Curling's roots are planted firmly in Scotland. That is where, in the sixteenth century, the world's first solid evidence of curling was discovered. There is little doubt that the game played on ice with stones originated and took hold in Scotland. Why else do you think so many of the game's traditions are associated with that wee country? The Scots clearly nurtured the game, improved it, established rules, turned it into a national pastime, and exported it to other countries.

Curling certainly suited the national character of the sports-loving Scotsman who enjoyed the outdoors and feats of strength. It is easy to understand why the wearer of the plaid would turn to heaving heavy stones on frozen lochs and tarns when winter's icy grip took hold of the country.

However plausible, Scotland's claim to the game is challenged by some curling historians. They like to point to the Netherlands, where an ice game, called "eisschiessen," appears in two paintings by the sixteenth-century Dutch master Pieter Bruegel, entitled *Hunters in the Snow* and *Winter Landscape with a Birdtrap*. "Eisschiessen" has been played in parts of Europe (primarily Bavaria and Austria) for centuries, and is still enjoyed today. It is played with a long "stick-like" handle on a rink approximately 33 to 60 yards (30 to 54 m) in length with footholds 20 to 60 yards (18 to 54 m) apart. The mark, or target, is a movable oak jack, just 4 inches (10 cm) high. The object of the game is to position your stick between the opponent's stick and the jack. Sounds a bit like curling to me.

It's interesting to note that the rudiments of stick delivery are much like those for today's curlers. The stick is delivered with a curling-like swing and touched down on the ice as smoothly as possible.

The word "curling" first appeared in print with the publication of an elegy written by Henry Adamson of Perth, Scotland, in 1630. However, the first hard evidence of the existence of curling stones was reported in Scotland's

Paisley Abbey in 1541. These early stones were known as "loofies," from the Scots word "loof," meaning "palm of the hand." They were flat-bottomed and shaped like a hand, and weighed a scant 5 pounds (2.3 kg). In later years, kuting stones were used. These were river rocks, some of them weighing up to 25 pounds (11.3 kg), with a notch cut in each for the thumb. Many examples of these kind of stones have been found in dried-out or drained Scottish lochs and ponds. The earliest find is dated 1511, and other, more advanced models, date between 1551 and 1611.

These stones are the keys to unlocking the mystery of the game's birthplace. Since in no other country have such early stones been discovered, the game played on ice with stones must have originated in Scotland.

You might say that, once out of the hacks in Scotland, curling refused to budge. It barely changed a whit over the next two centuries, largely because the dearth of roads in the country at the time kept the game local, with no pressure to improve the equipment. Nobody seemed concerned with finding better stones with which to play. A player simply chose stones from the nearby river, shore, or dyke—whatever shape took his fancy—and off he went.

It was gradually discovered, however, that some stones performed better than others. The first improvements were made by cutting finger grooves and thumb holes to give the player a better grip on the stone. A little smoothing of the bottom also made for a better glide.

The "loofie" may have been thrown with the motion used to skip a flat stone across water. Initially, there was no intention to give it a rotary motion so it could curl on the ice and draw around a guard. So, as mentioned earlier,

the name "curling" did not derive from the motion of a stone on its way
down the ice.

Where did the name come from? Nobody is completely sure, but it could
have been derived from the old verb "curr"—to make a low or hoarse murmuring
sound, which might have been the distinctive call of a running "loofie."

That explanation actually makes sense. Today, many curlers associate the
roar (as in the "roaring" game) to the sound of the stone rumbling down the ice.

The evolution of curling was tied directly to equipment—primarily the stones.

Imagine the difficulty playing with those early stones. Different shapes
and sizes meant that good shots were likely made by dumb luck. But,
through a natural progression, the stones used eventually became rounder
and heavier. As players discovered that more could be done with those types
of stones, the skill level increased, and gradually interest in the game began
to grow. Curling was on the move—from a pastime to a truly national sport.

Early clubs had difficulty in furnishing sufficient stones for their
members. The rules of most clubs suggested that, within a year, a new
member had to provide a stone or a pair of stones that would become the
property of the club.

Most stones were shaped from blocks and boulders by local masons,
which explains why there was such a diversity of materials, shapes, sizes,
and weights. Many were rough, and some had a dual purpose—serving as
loom weights to stretch the web for most of the year, and as curling stones
when the winter weather permitted. Some were decorated with carvings;
others were painted.

It wasn't until the third quarter of the nineteenth century that curling
took a giant leap forward with the emergence of the highly polished circular
stones players are familiar with today.

While we're at it, let's shatter one more curling myth. Granite was seldom used in the early manufacture of curling stones. In fact, stones of the late nineteenth and early twentieth centuries were made of almost every type of volcanic rock *except* granite. The largest source of material for curling stones from the middle of the nineteenth century was Ailsa Craig, a small, rocky, volcanic isle about 10 miles (16 km) off the southwest coast in Scotland, at the mouth of the Firth of Clyde. At one time nearly half of all of the curling stones in the world came from that island.

Times have changed. In the past thirty years nearly all new stones have been made of rock obtained from Trevor in Northern Wales and shipped to Scotland for manufacture.

The rules of the game were followed loosely. However, the number of players, the length of the ice surface, and the size of the rings varied from township to township. In some parts of Scotland, teams of three, five, seven, eight, or even nine players, each throwing a single stone, was the rule. In the Edinburgh area, you could expect to find four players per team, each throwing a pair of stones. The Royal Caledonian Curling Club was formed in 1838 to help standardize rules, but it wasn't until 1853 that the final holdouts adopted the modern rules.

Curling had always been a slippery game, in terms of its chancy nature and the difficulties oldtime curlers had keeping their feet on the ice. Various devices and contraptions were developed over time to solve that problem.

One of the earliest forms of artificial foothold was a tricker, or trigger—a simple piece of ironmongery with spikes that fixed it firmly to the ice, something like the modern hack. Another device was the crampit, or tramp, which was clamped or tied to the foot like the crampons iceclimbers use today. But you can imagine the damage this footwear did to the ice surface.

Various other later devices proved to be more practical. The founder of the Royal Caledonian, John Cairnie, invented the footiron, later known as the crampit, which was used throughout Scotland for many years. The crampit is a piece of sheet iron, 3 feet 9 inches (114 cm) long, by 9 inches (23 cm) wide, well punctured on both sides, and turned up about 1 inch (2.5 cm) on the end.

In many parts of the world where curlers and skaters share the same ice surface, a raised hack that can be installed and removed quickly is the foothold of choice. Canadians, however, have long preferred the sunken rubber hack.

Sweeping has been a big part of the game since the advent of stones with handles. The broom was deemed so important that many clubs set rules for its use, or fined members for appearing on the ice without it.

The earliest form was the broom cowe, made from green branches of broom tied with string. At some stage, it was replaced by the multi-use besom—it was used for sweeping floors in the summer, and for curling in the winter. The household besom was refined throughout the nineteenth

The very ancient and precise process of developing a curling stone at the factory in Mauchline, Scotland. First, square blocks supplied by the quarry are very roughly shaped by hand and a hole is drilled down the middle.

century and eventually whittled down to the width of a walking stick.

The brush replaced the Scottish besom in the 1920s. Canadians, however, did not part quite so easily with their beloved broom, and used it almost exclusively until the brush took over in the mid-1980s.

CANADA: THE GAME FLOURISHES

Curling's home and soul is in Scotland, where the game is woven into the very fabric of the country. But how great a game would it be if it appealed only to one nation? Like all great games, curling eventually spread and found a following in other countries. Today it is played around the globe, but nowhere has it flourished as magnificently as in Canada. Curling proved to be an ideal game for a new, spirited country.

It is a great irony that Quebec, the birthplace of curling in Canada, today has the smallest number of curlers per capita. Why the game hasn't thrived in La Belle Province is open to debate, but Quebec clearly is where curling took its first tentative steps on this side of the ocean.

The first Canadian curlers were soldiers of the 78th Highlanders shortly after the fall of Quebec in 1759. The regiment was commanded by Simon Fraser, Lord Lovat, and participated in the assault on the citadel. Lord Lovat was a young man and had probably tossed a few stones himself in his days in Inverness-shire, where he formed the regiment. As the story goes, Fraser's ingenious infantrymen, rather than be deprived of their beloved game, came up with the idea of melting down some cannon balls and fashioning iron facsimiles of curling stones. Canadian curling was born on the St. Charles River in 1760.

Other than as a little fun and a diversion for the soldiers, this isolated event had little impact on the development of curling in Canada. But it did prove one thing: iron worked as a reasonable substitute for stone.

The earliest reports of curling in the Canadian press appeared in Beauport, near Quebec City, in 1805. Similar games were occurring elsewhere, and by 1807 the first official club, the Royal Montreal, was formed. Members played on the St. Lawrence River and attempted to keep up some of the old Scottish traditions: they dined on salt beef and greens, and met every fortnight for a rousing match.

A second club was organized in Quebec City in 1821. Cast-iron stones continued to be used exclusively since no suitable rock could be found in Quebec to make proper stones. The iron stones were forged in Trois-Rivières, cast from a wooden model. Trois-Rivières, halfway between Montreal and Quebec City, was also the site in 1835 of the first game between the two clubs. It took the teams two days to cover the 80 miles (129 km) to Trois-Rivières because of heavy snowfall and lousy roads.

The development of curling in Ontario was slow. Communications were dreadful, and the province was sparsely populated, but that changed after Napoleon's defeat in 1815. The British government relaxed its emigration restrictions, and about 40,000 people poured into Ontario between 1816 and 1823. Most of the immigrants were Scots, and they brought the game with them. The first Ontario club was organized in Kingston in 1820.

Immigrants from Dumfries and Lanark started curling in Toronto around 1825, and, as luck would have it, many of them happened to be stone masons. Granite and whinstone found in the fields being cleared for cultivation were soon turned into curling stones. Where good stone was unavailable, inventive pioneers turned to hardwood blocks ringed with iron. These "stones" proved to be more than adequate, and today are valuable collectors' items.

Curling in eastern Canada experienced the same growing pains faced by the Scots in the eighteenth century—few roads, slow travel, small, scattered communities, and lack of continuity with teams casually formed. When Toronto played its biannual match with the Hamilton Thistles, the visiting

Left: The final stage: polishing to establish the stone's running edge.

Right: Tea time at the curling-stone factory in Mauchline, Scotland.

Left: Outdoor curling in the Swiss Alps.

Right: Outdoor curling is popular high in the Swiss Alps.

team had to allow three days for their opponents, a mere 55 miles (86 km) away, to arrive. They obviously loved the sport, because getting there was no fun. Players traveled in sleighs and wagons loaded with stones, brooms, and shovels, and had to suffer a day's journey on bumpy roads each way. Meanwhile, half the day of the match was spent shoveling snow off the rink.

News dispatches reached Canada in 1833 that the Royal Caledonian Club had been founded, and the Royal Montreal and Quebec curling clubs quickly applied for membership as the Quebec Association. In 1843 the two clubs were renamed the Canadian Branch of the Royal Caledonian Curling Club. For more than thirty years, they were Canada's governing body of curling, headquartered in Montreal.

The center of curling in Ontario was Toronto, where the first club was established in 1837. Numerous other clubs were forming in the province, but most weren't interested in joining the burgeoning national body in Quebec. Not only were distances too great, but Quebec insisted on using the irons and stones were in play in much of Ontario. It was difficult seeing the two sides ever compromising on the issue, but eventually they tried. They matched two teams a side in a special competition, one using granites, and the other irons. Alas, it was inconclusive: each side won with its own stones.

There were three times more clubs operating in Ontario than in Quebec at the time, yet the Ontario clubs did not have representatives on the Canadian branch for the development of rules or policy. So in 1874 the clubs of Ontario joined together and formed the Branch of the Province of Ontario of the Royal Caledonian Club.

The move established a precedent, and Ontario encouraged the Western provinces to form independent curling associations and to affiliate directly with the Royal Caledonian. Curling was also gaining a toehold in the Maritime provinces. The first two clubs to spring up in Nova Scotia were in Halifax in 1824 and in Pictou in 1829; Scottish coalminers had had the good sense to bring stones with them from the old country.

The Scots were everywhere starting up their game. Another group formed

During the opening of the 1988 Labatt Brier in Chicoutimi-Jonquiere, a team of actors were clad in clothing like that worn by early curlers in Quebec.

a club at St. John's, Newfoundland, in 1843. Scottish immigrants, however, had nothing to do with kick-starting the game in New Brunswick. That honor belonged to a journalist with the *Glasgow Herald* who wrote passionately about Scotland's Grand Match, held in 1854. The local readers needed no more encouragement. Suitably impressed, they imported stones and started a club the same year. The Royal Caledonian Curling Club once more was instrumental, helping the Atlantic region by providing medals for competition and offering valuable advice.

The Scots were not only sowing the seeds of the game in the east, but were also busy spreading them in the west, where the game found its most fertile ground. It was a natural sport on the Prairies, where the winters are long and harsh. Curling provided a spirited break from the chores of daily life.

The first settlers in Manitoba in 1812 were curlers who made rocks from oak blocks. Curling quickly became a passion there, and by 1888 Manitoba

Outdoor curling at Banff, Alberta, in 1899.

clubs outnumbered those in Quebec and Ontario combined. The Manitoba Branch of the Royal Caledonian Club was soon in place.

The spread of the game across the Prairies to the foothills of Alberta and beyond was steady. Curling clubs sprang up like mushrooms across the vast landscape. In Saskatchewan, many small clubs were formed within short distances so farmers would not have to travel too far to play. The early clubs in Saskatchewan, Alberta, and British Columbia were all affiliated with the Manitoba Branch, but they formed their own provincial associations between 1904 and 1906.

Curling was born as an outdoor game, played on ponds and rivers, but the game didn't come of age until it moved indoors. It was a necessity, especially on the Prairies, where prolonged cold snaps of thirty-below were not only unpleasant but also dangerous. It made good sense to get in out of the cold. The bigger clubs slowly began to build covered rinks, which offered, as a bonus, the chance to play at night.

Indoor curling started in Montreal with the first covered club in 1847, followed by Toronto (1859), Hamilton (1860), Ottawa (1868), and Winnipeg (1876). Canadians warmed up to the game. Club memberships increased so rapidly that, by the end of the century, the media and advertisers were starting to pay attention to this wonderful new form of recreation. Many of the kingpins of industry presented medals, prizes, and trophies at various bonspiels, and as a result the game attracted more curlers, and more money.

Bonspiels were beginning to be popular events. The 1888 Winnipeg bonspiel, for example, drew sixty-two teams from all parts of Canada and the United States to play in the indoor comfort of the Winnipeg Curling Club.

Pretty much all of Canadian curling was under some sort of cover by 1900. The small towns built wooden structures, while the larger cities often used brick buildings with room for four to six sheets of ice.

The method of making ice had a huge influence on the game. Although all the ice was natural, it was made by a skilled icemaker. The floor was made first, by removing topsoil and then covering the surface with 6 inches (15 cm) of well-compacted sand. At some rinks, 10-inch (25-cm) joists were laid across cedar sleepers, and the spaces between packed with ashes. A tongue-and-groove floor of white lead and oiled wood was laid on top. Ventilators at the floor and roof admitted cold air, and let warm air escape.

The actual ice was made much as it is today. The floor was sprayed with successive thin coats until the sheet was watertight. The ice was then given several successive floodings, each of small depth, to allow the water to reach its natural level before freezing. A final sprinkling of pebble and—voila!—it was game on.

Stones were also getting better all the time. Many curlers still imported Scottish stones, but most settlers made their own from the Scottish model.

Hacks replaced crampits at indoor rinks. The crampit had severe limitations. It was impossible for a player to deliver with anything except a stationary foot position. When curling moved indoors, Canadians opted for the simple hack; that would change the game in a big way. It was as if someone had opened the drapes and let the sunshine in. The hack completely altered the throwing technique, allowing a toe grip for the right foot and a different angle of delivery. Players eventually learned to move forward as the stone was delivered, and swing their left leg toward the target. Another important element of curling—the slide delivery—was born.

And so, from very humble beginnings in Quebec, curling was now on its way in Canada. But those early pioneers could never have imagined where the game was headed in the twentieth century, and the huge impact it would have as part of Canada's sporting mosaic.

THE ASSOCIATIONS: THE GAME GETS ORGANIZED

The Canadian Curling Association

Anything that takes more than a century to create must be worth waiting for, and I guess you can say that about the administration of curling in Canada. It took a long time for a national curling association to be formed in Canada, but today the sport is in fine hands. The Canadian Curling Association has been taking care of the interests of curlers across the country since 1935.

So what took so long for curling to come together as one national body? It wasn't lack of trying. Attempts were made as early as 1851 to form a national association, but every proposal was scuttled or abandoned because it was deemed unworkable.

One of the first serious attempts was pitched in 1927, when the New Brunswick Branch of the Royal Caledonian Curling Club sent a letter to the other provincial associations in Canada suggesting the time was ripe for a Dominion Curling Association. The Brier was already into its second year, and there was need for a Canada-wide standard of rules. Delegates met in Toronto, talked a lot, but in the end nothing happened.

The clouds finally began to break in 1931 at the annual meeting of the Ontario Curling Association (OCA), where the call for a national body became louder. The OCA president was asked to appoint a committee to meet with representatives from the other provinces to see if they could finally reach common ground. Several resolutions were put in place to unite all curlers in Canada and agree on uniform rules of play. The proposals were accepted in 1931, but it wasn't until 1935 that a draft constitution was agreed to by all associations. Finally, the Dominion Curling Association was at work, and just in the nick of time. There were 12 associations operating in the country, with 613 clubs and a registration of 25,000 curlers. The association changed its name to the Canadian Curling Association (CCA) during the 1967–68 season.

The women took longer to get organized, and it wasn't until 1960, following their first-ever national championship, that the Canadian Ladies Curling Association (CLCA) was born.

But several important changes were still to come. Curl Canada was created in 1974 as a joint venture of the CCA and CLCA. The new organization, funded in part by the federal government (Sport Canada), was established to develop skill instruction and set technical standards. Curl Canada trained instructors, who, in turn, conducted courses to improve the caliber and participation of curling at all levels. Curl Canada also conducted seminars on topics such as icemaking and the building and operation of curling clubs, and promoted the sport across the country through manuals and films.

Three separate bodies were now governing curling in Canada, but the political structure was to change dramatically in 1989, when the men's CCA, the CLCA, and Curl Canada were amalgamated to form the Canadian Curling Association. One body, one voice would now speak for curling in Canada.

The CCA today governs the sport in three key areas: championships, high performance, and development. The CCA is responsible every year for the organization and operation of the five Canadian championships (Mixed, Seniors, Juniors, Scott Tournament of Hearts, and Labatt Brier) and two world championships (when hosted by Canada). It pays many of the bills for these events; provides officials, statisticians, and ice technicians; and deals directly with the media. Still, these events are staged largely by dedicated host committees and their small armies of volunteers, without whom these events could not be held. The CCA's professional staff and volunteer officials are on hand for all championships to ensure their successful operation.

The CCA also selects and trains teams for the Olympics, conducts National Team programs, and develops Level IV and V coaches.

The CCA runs a series of programs aimed at retaining existing curlers and the recruitment of new players. Development programs give the CCA a

direct link to some 1,140 affiliated curling clubs, 28 provincial and territorial associations, and the 1.2 million Canadians who play the sport each year.

The Calgary Curling Club, a typical modern Canadian curling club.

The United States Curling Association

Bud Somerville, perhaps the greatest curler to come out of the United States, is a wonderful example of the sport in his country. The United States doesn't produce a lot of curlers for a country its size. The game is established mostly in the northern states, and the sports-minded American media still treat the game with merely passing interest. But the United States still produces some world-class curlers, like Somerville, who is a credit to a strong national association and dedicated players. It hasn't hurt the Americans to be next door to Canada, the largest and strongest curling nation in the world.

Curling is a winter sport, so it's not surprising the game thrives in the north. Unfortunately, it is virtually invisible in the south. Curling is played in 26 states by approximately 15,000 curlers in 135 clubs across the country, the largest concentration being in Wisconsin, where 4,000 enjoy the game. Minnesota is next, with 3,000 curlers, 700 of them registered with a club in St. Paul. Curling is also enjoyed along the east coast, and clubs have sprung up in California, Washington, and Alaska.

The Scots—who else?—were responsible for bringing the game to the United States. There is no written evidence of curling prior to 1832, but since several hundred Scottish communities were scattered through the colony before the War of Independence (1775–83), it is assumed some informal curling took place before the formation of the first club.

The game officially arrived with a thud when a group of Scottish farmers who were migrating by boat through the wilds of Michigan were wrecked on the shore of Lake St. Clair. The winter offered excellent curling, so they met at the house of Dr. Robert Burns in January 1832 and formed a club. They sawed "rocks" from hickory trees, shaped them, and began play. There is a record of curling in New York in the 1830s, and, down the coast, the New England Club of Boston was formed in 1839. Curlers were playing on the Milwaukee River with wooden blocks in 1843, and formed a club two years later. Many of these early clubs played with wooden blocks, although the Chicago Club (formed in 1854) used real stones picked from the shores of Lake Michigan.

The first international bonspiel was held on Lake Erie in 1865 at Black Rock, near Buffalo, and thousands of spectators showed up to take in the festivities. It was a lively scene, with flags flying, skaters dashing about, and the crowd cheering.

The sport grew quickly, and soon twelve clubs, nearly all from the east, joined together in 1867 to form the Grand National Curling Club of America. The club did not initially affiliate with the Royal Caledonian but did use its rules. As the Western states were settled, more clubs joined the Grand National, including three Canadian clubs (the Scots, it appeared, had little regard for international boundaries).

As the sport became more popular, the Grand National Club split into two separate groups—fourteen clubs north and east of Ohio broke away and formed the North-Western Curling Association. Both of the groups remained strong, and continued to build rinks and compete in local and international matches. Curling's future in the United States looked bright. Then disaster fell.

The First World War, the Great Depression, and twenty years of warm winter weather left the Eastern clubs in shambles. Curling in the area was saved only by the gradual introduction of artificial ice rinks in the late 1920s and early 1930s. The North-Western Curling Association was wiped out, but a few individual clubs did manage to survive.

Club numbers started to swell again after the Second World War, and for the first time curling stretched across the entire country. The U.S. Men's Association was founded in 1958 and became the governing body for men's curling. The U.S. Women's Association (founded in 1947) joined the men in 1976 and the U.S. Curling Association was born. The association annually administrates national championships for men, women, juniors, and mixed curlers.

The World Curling Federation

It was only intended to be a friendly, two-nation competition for something called the Scotch Cup. But Regina's Ernie Richardson never stepped on the

Three of the famous Richardsons: Wes, Sam, and Ernie during one of their four Scotch Cup wins.

ice for anything friendly, at least not with a curling broom in his hands. Richardson, one of the greatest curlers produced in Canada, meant business every time he played, and the Scotch Cup was no different.

The Scotch Cup is an important touchstone to the past because it is the spark that ignited international curling and led to the world curling championships we know today. And Richardson, the tall, refined skip from Regina, had an immeasurable impact on making it happen. His popularity and his team's skill forced other curling countries to stand up and take notice of international curling's huge potential.

The world curling scene is a whole lot different today from what it was in Richardson's era. Under the auspices of the World Curling Federation, the game is played in thirty-four countries around the world and is a full-fledged member of the Olympic family.

Richardson could never have dreamed of such growth when he squared off against Scotland's Willie Young in 1959 in the first meaningful international competition since the first Winter Olympic Games in Chamonix, France, in 1924. Richardson and his family team were outstanding, sweeping the series in five straight games. The series was an instant hit, and international curling was back in business. Richardson also won the Scotch Cup the following year, and by then there was a groundswell of interest. The United States joined in 1961, and before long other countries came calling. In the next few years, Sweden, Norway, Switzerland, France, and Germany were competing for the Cup.

The need for an international body became necessary, and in 1965 six countries (Scotland, Canada, the United States, Sweden, Norway, and Switzerland) formed an international committee as a division of the Royal

Canada's Rick Lang and Bill Tetley sweep the 117-pound Jubilee stone at the opening of the 1975 Air Canada Silver Broom in Perth, Scotland.

Caledonian Curling Club. The committee would later become the International Curling Federation (ICF).

The game grew and prospered under the ICF. The Scotch Cup became the Air Canada Silver Broom in 1968 and was granted official sanction as the world curling championships. Other new world championships were developed and endorsed over the next two decades, including the world junior men's (1975), world ladies' (1979), and world junior ladies' (1988). The four events have now been distilled to two: the World Curling Championships (WCC) and the World Junior Curling Championships (WJCC).

The biggest development, however, was about to come. The ICF became the World Curling Federation (WCF) in 1991, and after a couple of appearances as a demonstration sport in the Olympics, curling received full-medal status in 1992.

Today, the WCF comprises thirty-four member nations, with some 1.2 million curlers. Canada accounts for almost one million of the total.

The WCF has a four-part mandate:

1. To represent curling internationally and facilitate the growth of the sport through a network of member nations;

2. To formulate rules of the sport for world competitions and all other competitions approved by the WCF;

3. To conduct world curling competitions; and

4. To provide cooperation and mutual understanding among member nations and to unite curlers throughout the world.

The Game

Thousands of people around the world curl, but ask any of them why they started playing the game and the answer is often very vague. Canadians usually fall back on the old cliché about thinking "it would make the winter go by quicker." But there is much, much more to it than that.

Adults may pick up the game because their office or church has started a league, or they saw it on television and it looked interesting enough to try. Kids get involved because their parents take them to the rink, or a school or junior program has been organized. Curlers have also been known to counsel their non-curling friends about the merits of the game, thereby inviting new devotees to pick up the brush.

Whatever led them to start, many curlers stick with the game because it is fun to play, good exercise, affordable, and provides a social element missing in most other sports. For others, it is all of that and more. Curling has its elite level of players who compete for the opportunity to go as far up the competitive ladder as the Olympic Games. But they are the exceptions. The majority of curlers around the world play for the sheer enjoyment of the game, and the sociability that comes with it.

And why not? There are so many facets of the game that are appealing. It is, for instance, a satisfying game because the rudiments of curling can be learned fairly quickly. There are many curling programs available now that can get a novice curler up to speed and playing with some degree of competence. Curling is also unusual among active sports because you don't have to be a great athlete to compete. A person can be lacking youth, brawn, speed of foot, suppleness of muscle, and other athletic virtues, and still be a pretty fair curler.

Mind you, that's always been a knock against curling. People who don't play or understand it pass curling off as more recreation than sport—a pastime requiring little, if any, athletic skill. But they're wrong. Curling is played at its highest level by skilled athletes who have also been very good at other sports. You won't find many paunchy, out-of-shape curlers playing at the world level.

Curling can be a humbling game. It looks to be an easy sport to play, and yet it is one of the hardest to play consistently well. The fact is, the moment curlers think they have the game aced and start playing with the champs, they discover they've still got a long way to go in the skill and strategy departments.

But that doesn't stop any curler from being an "expert." Anybody who has played the game on a regular basis is convinced they know it inside out. That's why so many of them also love watching the high-profile events. It is a chance for them to second-guess a skip's strategy.

One of the charms of curling is the uniqueness of its "playing field." No two sheets of curling ice are identical. Each sheet possesses its own distinct and recognizable nuances, and a big challenge in the game is to figure them out before the opponent can. Ice conditions have improved dramatically over the years, with new technology. Many of the rustic conditions Grandpa used to face have been virtually eliminated today. But there will always be variables in ice conditions, an element of the game that has long fascinated curlers.

Curling is a game men and women can carry through life. There is no debating, though, that the earlier a person takes up the game, the easier it is to develop the proper fundamentals. The delivery, for instance, is a disciplined exercise in coordination (much like a golf swing) that can be perfected only through practice. It's a form of muscle memory that must be practiced over and over again. Talk to any of the world's best players and you will be told of endless hours put in throwing practice stones. They didn't become good overnight.

Starting young is a key, but there have been plenty of cases of men and women picking up the game late in life and still attaining a measure of proficiency. A classic example is Lloyd Gunnlaugson of Winnipeg, who never really took up the game seriously until he was well into his forties. He went on to represent Manitoba at the Brier and won three Canadian senior men's championships while in his fifties.

Curling certainly provides some interesting situations. Just think about it: what other sport makes it possible for your average, garden-variety competitor to challenge the best in the world? Will the high handicapper down at Hack and Slice Country Club ever get the chance to play Tiger Woods in a meaningful game? Of course not. But those kinds of situations come up in curling all the time. It is the uniqueness of curling in Canada that the defending men's champion is often forced to start virtually from scratch the following season. That may be tough for the defending champ, but imagine the thrill it gives the club curler to face one of the best in the world in zone playdowns.

It is not uncommon for some of these Davids to beat the Goliaths along the way. Curling lore is filled with stories of big-name curlers who were humbled by some unknown in a cashspiel or club playdown.

Curling is also a sport where women can compete with, and against, the men. You don't have to be a behemoth with bulging muscles to play the game. And, unlike in golf, women curlers don't need any artificial advantage, such as playing off the women's tees, to level the playing field.

It's not heresy to suggest that Sandra Schmirler's Regina team could compete against, and beat, many of the world's top men's teams.

Don't think so? Consider this. Many sports fans may remember the classic challenge tennis match between the game's ultimate hustler, Bobby Riggs, and women's great Billie Jean King in the early 1970s. It was billed "The Battle of the Sexes" and held in the Houston Astrodome. The event was big stuff on television and brought the nation's attention to the quality of play in women's pro tennis.

But how many people remember a similar match in curling? You could look it up. Saskatoon's Vera Pezer, the reigning Canadian women's champion, played Orest Meleschuk of Winnipeg, the world men's champion that year, in a one-game challenge match in 1972 on the weekly "CBC Curling Classic." It was the first time women's curling was showcased on network television, and most people expected The Big O to crush the woman from Saskatchewan. It never happened. Pezer shocked Meleschuk in the game played in Winnipeg, and in the space of a few hours women's curling had won some newfound respect.

Pezer never put much stock in that game. "He didn't take us seriously," she said later. "At a press conference before the game he asked us if we played takeouts or just draws. He curled poorly. All it meant is we could beat a hungover male skip." Still, that game was significant in proving a certain equality of the sexes.

True companionship flourishes on a curling team, as it does in few other sports. Competitive teams break up all the time as skips look for the "right combination of players" to win, but they are the exception. Most teams are formed because players simply want to play with each other. Many friendships made in the sport are lifelong.

Of course, curling's roots are in the social aspect. In what other game are the pleasures of sociability woven so naturally with the pleasures of an athletic contest. Anybody who has curled has also enjoyed the social aspect of the game afterward—a post-game beverage in the lounge upstairs to dissect what just transpired on the ice. Whether this is a good thing or bad can be debated, for there are many stories of curlers who partied too hearty. There is no better party than one put on by curlers.

The best aspects of curling come alive and flourish at the Labatt Brier. It is Canada's showcase curling event, and likely the biggest and best party in sports.

The Brier is often called "an extraordinary event played by ordinary Canadians." I don't know if I agree completely with that. The Brier is an extraordinary event, but what's so ordinary about some of the people who have played in it? Curlers such as Paul Gowsell, Matt Baldwin, Don Duguid, Hec Gervais, Ed Werenich, Russ Howard, and Guy Hemmings, among others, have all left indelible marks on the game and the event. Brier lore is filled with stories about these characters.

I like to think of the Brier as an extraordinary event played by extraordinary individuals, many of whom you will get to know better later in this book.

The "Purple Heart" has been the most cherished Brier trophy for participants at the Canadian men's curling championship since 1927.

The Macdonald Brier Tankard was symbolic of Brier supremacy from 1927 until 1979.

The sponsor of the first fifty Briers, Macdonald Tobacco, invited the twenty-two former winning skips to the final Macdonald Brier at Ottawa in 1979. Front row, left to right: Gordon Campbell, Ontario, 1936; Ken Watson, Manitoba, 1935, 1942, 1949; Ab Gowanlock, Manitoba, 1938, 1953; Billy Rose, Alberta, 1946; Jimmy Welsh, Manitoba, 1947; Frenchy D'amour, B.C., 1948; Tom Ramsay, Northern Ontario, 1950. Middle row: Don Oyler, Nova Scotia, 1951; Matt Baldwin, Alberta, 1954, 1957, 1958; Garnet Campbell, Saskatchewan, 1955; Ernie Richardson, Saskatchewan, 1959, 1960, 1962, 1963; Hec Gervais, Alberta, 1961, 1974; Terry Braunstein, Manitoba, 1965; Ron Northcott, Alberta, 1966, 1968, 1969; Alf Phillips, Ontario, 1967. Back row: Don Duguid, Manitoba, 1970, 1971; Orest Meleschuk, Manitoba, 1972; Harvey Mazinke, Saskatchewan, 1973; Bill Tetley, Northern Ontario, 1975; Jack McDuff, Newfoundland, 1976; Jim Ursel, Quebec, 1977; Ed Lukowich, Alberta, 1978. Missing from the photo is Barry Fry, 1979.

Yes, they lead ordinary lives. They may be car salesmen, postal workers, couriers, doctors, or farmers in their workaday lives, but get them under curling's brightest spotlight in March and they become special individuals. They are a big reason for the lasting success of the Brier and why it remains one of Canada's greatest sporting attractions.

The Brier is one of the rare, genuine examples of Canadiana, a sports extravaganza that brings the fans, players, officials, and media together unlike any other event. It has been held at least once in every province, from the rocky outcrop in St. John's, Newfoundland, to the tulip beds of Victoria, British Columbia, and in every town it has played there are memories.

The Brier is something of a contradiction. It is a slick, major spectacle on the Canadian sports scene, rivaling the Grey Cup in stature, but at the same time it has built its appeal on tradition and a sense of consistency. The trappings, the pageantry, and the bagpipes are all part of it. The fans will tell you. They journey from across the country year after year to roar their approval, as some of the most skilled players in the world compete for the men's curling championship of Canada. I may be biased, but I believe the Brier has had some of the most memorable moments in Canadian sports.

Part of the allure of the Brier is that, unlike other sports, it is open to any Canadian and is a completely amateur affair. There are no professionals at the Brier, at least not yet. Every Canadian can throw his hat in the ring and take his best shot. There is still a quaint innocence about the event. A few years ago, Quebec third Dan Lemery had to miss the opening ceremonies because he couldn't get anyone to take over his bread truck delivery route. Then there is Don McKenzie, former lead of the Pat Ryan team from

Edmonton that won the 1989 Brier. Then next day he was back at work as a plumber, standing knee deep in water.

The Brier is also one of sport's great parties. It is an opportunity to wear a funny hat, to trade pins, wave a provincial flag, and make unending conversation with the fan next to you about the merits of corn broom over brush. The nature of the gathering remains the same year after year. Saskatchewan people always travel to watch their farming brothers represent the province. Newfoundlanders always make everyone else drink Screech and kiss a real fish. Fans from Nova Scotia show up with their noses painted blue.

But the Brier is considered something more than just a chance to wake up 1,000 miles away from home wearing somebody else's raincoat. It has been, and always will be, about curling and deciding Canada's best men's team.

For many curlers, it's a lifetime passion to get to "The Show." Hang around them for a while and you'll appreciate their passion. Stan Austman, a former schoolboy champion from Saskatchewan, spent most of his adult curling career trying to get to the Brier. He finally made it as a fifth man on Eugene Hritzuk's 1985 Brier team from Saskatoon and, as luck would have it, got his one and only chance to play when a regular on the Saskatoon team took sick. I remember Stan, now in his fifties, crying like a baby after the

Left: The program from the 1979 Brier, with the signatures of all the former champion skips.

Right: David M. Stewart, president of Macdonald Tobacco, the sponsor of the first fifty Briers, at the 1977 event in Montreal.

The host committee has been the driving force behind each and every Brier.

game because he was so happy. He had finally realized his dream, if only for one game.

The Brier has always been a great vehicle for unity in Canada. The best example came in Kamloops in 1996, when Quebec's team, skipped by Don Westphal, climbed up on stage at the Brier Patch—party headquarters— between draws in the middle of the week. It was the first Brier after an endless series of referendums on sovereignty in Quebec. The personable team members announced they'd like to present a special gift to the crowd, and proceeded to sing "O Canada." There wasn't a dry eye in the house. I always think fans leave the Brier more enlightened, more appreciative of the likes and dislikes of their neighbors.

Almost from the beginning, the Brier was intended to bring the East and the West closer together. It was really the brainchild of Winnipeg's George J. Cameron, who envisioned one event that would foster curling and friendship in Canada and help unify the country.

Curling is not only a great game to play, it is just as fascinating and entertaining to watch when the best in the world are involved. That could explain why the Brier and Scott Tournament of Hearts are major sporting attractions in Canada, and why they are a smashing success on television.

Curling on television is nothing new, of course. It's been a staple for many years in Canada and has always had pretty good audience numbers. But now it's absolutely huge. The final of the Brier consistently attracts a television audience in excess of 1.4 million, based on a quarter-hour rating

The ceremonial rock team at the 1986 Labatt Brier in Kitchener-Waterloo: the skip, Prime Minister Brian Mulroney, with sweepers Ed Werenich and Al Hacker, and thrower Hector Gervais (back to camera).

period and a reach of 3 million. (Reach, a CBC statistic, is the number of people who have tuned in to the telecast for at least one minute.) In 1997, curling held four of the top fifteen positions of sports properties on Canadian television, including the Brier, at No. 6. Figure skating and curling were the only amateur sports to rank in the top fifteen of the survey.

Canadians obviously love to watch curling on television. There are more viewers than people actually playing the game. In fact, there are people who have never thrown a rock in competition who wouldn't miss a telecast. The question is: why?

Certainly, it's very good programming, a testament to the job done by two Canadian networks, the CBC and the Sports Network (TSN). Curling is perfect for television because it can provide tight, close-up shots of the competitors. It's a game of "faces." You could also say it's a game of voices, too, because players (at the Canadian championships) all wear microphones. This allows the viewer at home to feel part of the action on the ice. There is no other sport on television that provides this type of intriguing involvement on a continuous basis.

Unfortunately, curling on television seems to be a Canadian phenomenon. Coverage pretty much stops at the Canadian border. Curlers were utterly dismayed by the total lack of coverage the U.S. networks gave their sport at the 1998 Olympic Winter Games in Nagano, Japan. Americans in general do not understand the game and its nuances, which may be why the U.S. networks stayed away from curling at the Olympics.

Left: The media have always supported the Brier in big numbers and full coverage. The media bench at the 1963 Brier in Brandon is shown above.

Right: The fans at the Brier have always been an integral part of the event. Here, over 17,000 curling fans watch the action of the 1997 Labatt Brier at the Canadian Airlines Saddledome in Calgary.

Curling, for the most part, is an amateur sport—most curlers play for the love of the game. Competitive curlers are also in it for the glory—the chance to represent their province, state, or country. But more and more competitive curlers are starting to look at the money aspect of their sport. Someday there will likely be a pro tour, where players make a decent living from the sport. Calgary's Ed Lukowich, a former Canadian champion, hopes the World Curling Tour (WCT) is the framework for such a professional association.

Lukowich had a vision in 1993. He saw a number of independent cash bonspiels being held across Canada every fall, and thought it made sense to tie them together in a tour. He asked various bonspiel organizers to buy into the WCT idea and charge each curler entering the event a modest fee. Players could then earn tour points, with the top thirty-two teams competing for the WCT championship at the end of the cashspiel season (around the middle of December).

The idea has had its growing pains but made a major breakthrough in 1998. It could hold the key to the tour's future. The WCT, now under the control of the Canadian Curling Players' Association, pulled together an operating arrangement with CTV Sportsnet and International Management Group (IMG), a sports marketing and management agent. IMG came to the table with a minimum guarantee of $10,000 first-place money for a number of selected events, and Sportsnet agreed to provide Sunday-to-Monday television coverage during the fall. Monday Night Football worked, so why not Monday Night Curling?

The three-year agreement among IMG, Sportsnet, and the WCT could enable the fledgling tour to establish itself as a legitimate player in the big scheme of things. The money is starting to get serious. Some teams are pulling in more than $50,000 during the three-month season, and that's been enough to draw the attention of Revenue Canada, which is threatening to tax top money-winning players.

Money, though, does not motivate the vast majority of people who take up the wonderful game of curling. For them, the lure is the same as it has been for generations of curlers. It is fun, pure and simple.

THE OLYMPICS

Curling in the Olympic Games. Who could have imagined?

That's not to say curling doesn't belong in the Games. It does. But merit alone doesn't automatically get a sport into the exclusive Olympic family. If you could understand the politics involved and the mountains that have to be climbed to get a sport into the Olympics, you'd realize the daunting task curling faced getting through the front door.

The roarin' game was part of the first Olympics in Chamonix, France, in 1924, but was more or less dropped after that. I had long held a vision of curling again being in the Games. Some people thought I was nuts. Curling in the Olympics? It will never happen, they'd say with a snicker. I'd heard it all before. Every sport has its detractors, and curling is not without its braying pack of naysayers who view the sport as too passive, and as more recreation than legitimate sport.

As I would later find out, some of the most vocal people against curling's acceptance into the Games were influential Canadians, and one in particular. Still, this was a game worth fighting for, and the thought of curling in the Olympics got my old competitive juices flowing. I wasn't alone. My longtime friend and CCA board member Ray Kingsmith of Calgary shared my passion and vision. The Kingfish, as he was known to all his friends in curling, was also a scrapper when it came to the best interests of the game. He also thought there were new vistas for curling to conquer, and the Olympics was the top of the mountain.

Left: Chamonix, France, 1924: the British curling team, led by their captain, Col. T.S.G.H. Robertson Aikman, at the opening of the Winter Olympic Games.

Right: The curling rink at the Winter Olympic Games, Chamonix, France, 1924.

Together we were about to embark on a wonderful adventure that would land curling right smack in the middle of the Games as a medal sport. The Kingfish never got to see the project to its end. He died of cancer before curling was fully accepted, but his love of curling, his hard work, and his good humor buoyed us all as we struggled to get the job done.

Curling was granted full medal status in June 1992, but the work to get it there began a full decade earlier. It started with a simple phone call to Kingsmith at his home in Calgary.

"What do you think, Raybo," I asked, "of curling getting demonstration status in Calgary?" The Alberta city had been awarded the 1988 Olympic Winter Games, and it seemed like curling, such a big part of Canadian winter sports, would be a perfect fit. Kingsmith had been thinking the same thing. "Let's go for it," he agreed. The wheels were set in motion.

Those early days were real eye-openers for most of us in curling. We were neophytes to this Olympic business of backroom deals and high-stakes politicking, even though a lot of us were well schooled in the politics of our own sport. But this was the big time.

I remember our first exploratory meeting, on December 7, 1982, with Brian Murphy, vice-president of sports for the Calgary Olympic Organizing Committee (OCO). Murphy was friendly and informative and laid the facts out on the table for the two of us. Curling, he pointed out, wasn't the only sport banging on the door to get into the Olympics. Ski-orienteering, freestyle skiing, short-track speed-skating, sled-dogging and ballroom dancing were also being considered for demonstration status. And only three would be selected. They weren't the best odds, although we were certain that curling deserved to get in.

Our chance came on August 22, 1983, when we were asked to make a verbal presentation to the executive board of the OCO. What they wanted to know was why curling should be a demonstration sport, what it would do for the Games locally and internationally, and would the financial returns from curling in the Olympics be significant?

It's good to have friends in curling. We put together a video presentation with the help of Bob Moir of the CBC and it, along with written documentation,

Sweden, Great Britain, and France demonstrate curling during the first Olympic Winter Games in 1924 at Chamonix, France.

answered those three questions and a whole lot more. We must have impressed somebody, because it was later announced that curling (men's and women's), along with short-track speedskating and freestyle skiing, would be the three demonstration sports in the 1988 Winter Games.

We were in, sort of, but these were anxious times. The long-term goal was to get curling into the Olympics as a full-fledged medal sport, so Calgary was crucial. What if we fumbled the ball? Curling, we realized, had to put its best foot forward or all could be lost for the future.

There was plenty of work to do. We still needed the blessing of the International Curling Federation (ICF). An Olympic committee, working in conjunction with the Canadian Curling Association, needed to be put together to run the event for the OCO. And there seemed to be more questions than answers. What countries would compete in the Games? Where would the event be held? Who would be in charge?

The Canadian gold medal winners in demonstration curling on the podium at the 1988 Winter Olympics in Calgary. From the left: Linda Moore, Lindsay Sparkes, Debbie Jones-Walker, Penny Ryan, and Patti Vande.

The Olympic committee was put together in the spring of 1986 at the ICF annual meeting. It comprised president Phillip Dawson of Scotland, Harvey Mazinke of Regina (North America), Pierre Thuring of Switzerland (Europe), and Winnipeg's Ina Light (women's curling). The committee's first key decision was to settle on a format: Canada plus the top seven nations from the 1987 world curling championships would compete in Calgary.

We made some mistakes along the way and I believe they cost curling some precious brownie points with the International Olympic Committee (IOC). None of us were really schooled in IOC protocol. We were naively led to believe that, if our sport looked impressive in its debut in Calgary and we lobbied the right people, curling would be on the fast track to the Olympics. But we neglected to take care of some important business to ensure its acceptance as a full-medal sport.

For one thing, the ICF was unaware of a fundamental IOC guideline that required twenty-five member nations to compete in the sport on three

Canada's bronze-medal-winning men's team at the 1988 Winter Olympics. From the left: Ed Lukowich, John Ferguson, Ncil Houston, Brent Syme, and Wayne Hart.

continents. Curling at this stage did not have the numbers. How had that key criterion slipped by us?

Nevertheless, we did a bang-up job in Calgary, despite a mind-boggling ticket fiasco at the Max Bell Arena, the site for curling. The Games were a tremendous hit in southern Alberta. Curling, as expected, was overshadowed by the major events such as hockey, figure skating, downhill skiing, and speedskating, but it did grab its share of the media spotlight.

The ticket snafu was embarrassing, though. It was hard to believe many fans were turned away at Max Bell because of apparent sellouts, and yet the building was nearly empty. To this day the reason for the confusion has not been explained.

The high we all experienced after Calgary was short-lived. Curling did not receive a favorable nod from one of the key people, IOC Director of Sport, Walter Troeger of Germany. He made it clear he wasn't happy with curling's status in Calgary and indicated a demonstration sport would never enjoy such a lofty position again.

These were lousy times. The Olympic push was beset with problems, and it looked like curling's acceptance into the Olympic family was going down the tubes. Then the worst news of all. My good friend Raybo fell ill shortly after the Games and passed away May 3, 1988. I was devastated. He had been like a second father, and many times had helped me through the political jungle of the curling world. It was Kingsmith who had actually

The Canadian bronze medal winners in demonstration curling on the podium at the 1992 Winter Olympics in Prolagnan-La-Vanoise, France. From the left: Elaine Dagg-Jackson, Karri Wilms, Melissa Soligo, Jodie Sutton, Julie Sutton.

Page 46: The theme of the 1983 Silver Broom was the "Silver World," marking the twenty-fifth anniversary of world curling. The champions from the first twenty-four years were: (back row, left to right) Bud Somerville, U.S.A., 1965, 1974; Barry Naimark (for the late Lyall Dagg), Canada, 1964; Ron Northcott, Canada, 1966, 1968, 1969; Al Hackner, Canada, 1982; Jurg Tanner, Switzerland, 1981; Hec Gervais, Canada, 1961; (middle row) Bob Nichols, U.S.A., 1978; Kristian Soerum, Norway, 1979; Rick Folk, Canada, 1980; Chuck Hay, Scotland, 1967; Ernie Richardson, Canada, 1959, 1960, 1962, 1963; (front row) Don Duguid, Canada, 1970, 1971; Orest Meleschik, Canada, 1972; Kjell Oscarius, Sweden, 1973; Otto Danielli, Switzerland, 1975; Ragnar Kamp, Sweden, 1977. Missing is Bruce Roberts, U.S.A., 1976.

opened the door for me to get involved with the Canadian Curling Association in 1974, when he introduced me to newly elected third vice-president Herb Millham. The CCA had decided to become involved in the business of developing an instructors' program, and Kingsmith convinced Millham that I was the man to do the job.

Kingsmith was a straight-up breath of fresh air who said it the way it was. Not everyone always agreed with him, but he had a passion for curling that burned within like an inferno and pushed him to continually strive to improve the sport. I'm sure our shared love of curling and desire to make it better was the reason we became such good friends.

The failure of curling to address the twenty-five-nations, three-continents requirement would come back to haunt us. Our sport didn't meet the IOC criteria and we were denied full-medal entry into the next two winter Olympics, in Albertville, France (1992), and Lillehammer, Norway (1994). But they threw us a bone. Curling would remain a demo sport in Albertville.

So it was back to the drawing board. The torch was passed to retiring COA technical director Jack Lynch, and Gunther Hummelt of Austria, to lead curling to the Promised Land. A new plan was mapped out under Lynch's guiding hand, and it was full-speed ahead.

The ICF formed an international development committee by the summer of 1989, with Hummelt as its chairman. Later that year, the ICF joined the General Assembly of International Sports Federations (GAISF), which immediately requested a name change, since both canoeing and carting also used the initials ICF. Curling would now become the World Curling Federation (WCF).

But that was the easy part. Getting curling's numbers up to twenty-five countries on three continents was going to be tough, and we knew it. And those goals had to be reached prior to the 1991 session (General Assembly)

Canada's gold medal winners at the 1998 Winter Olympics in Nagano, Japan. From the left: Atina Ford, Marcia Gudereit, Joan McCusker, Jan Betker, and Sandra Schmirler.

of the IOC, when the host city for the 1998 Olympic Winter Games would be selected.

The first job was to get the Pacific region into the world curling championships without altering the present ten-team format. As expected, the debate was long and complex, mostly because an entry from the Pacific would mean one less spot for North America or Europe. Nobody wanted to give up ground. It took about three years to hammer out the details, but eventually the current system was passed. It gave seven or eight entries to Europe, one or two to North America and a single entry to the Pacific. The system was in place in time to provide the Pacific with entries in both the men's and women's demonstration events in Albertville.

Hummelt, now the WCF president, tackled the bigger job of recruiting new curling countries. He personally did all the spadework to bring Czechoslovakia, Hungary, Bulgaria, and Belgium into the fold, and negotiated tirelessly with Romania, Yugoslavia, Argentina, Turkey, and Russia, among others. He also made preliminary overtures to Korea.

The basic strategy was to find a curling "attaché" resident in the target country who could coordinate the introduction of the game and build toward a

curling branch. Plans were established for a WCF novice clinic to be held for thirty-two or more people in the target countries, using two or three sets of curling stones that would be left behind on a renewable-loan basis. This process brought countries such as Czechoslovakia and New Zealand into the fold.

The addition of New Zealand, Andorra, Liechtenstein, Iceland, and Mexico brought WCF membership up to twenty-five countries by March 1991. A group from the Virgin Islands applied in the summer of 1991, and Russia wasn't far behind. Curling finally had the requisite numbers, but would the

IOC accept it? There were no guarantees. Acceptance rests on the free vote of its ninety-odd individual members. All applications are filtered through a program commission before the general membership ever sees them. The program commission consists of about a half-dozen IOC members, supplemented with an appointee from each of the international federations, the national Olympic committees, and the Athletes' Commission.

The program commission rejected curling's bid—not once, but twice. The commission, chaired at that time by Vitaly Smirnov of Russia, panned

The joy of victory and the pain of defeat: Andreas Haenni and Patrik Loertscher of Switzerland contrast with a triumphant Randy Ferbey of Canada at the 1989 men's world championship in Milwaukee, Wisconsin.

The four-time women's world champions (1992, 1995, 1998, 1999) from Sweden: alternate Margaretha Lindahl, lead Elisabeth Persson, second Louise Marmont, third Katarina Nyberg, and skip Elisabeth Gustafson.

curling, claiming it was not really a sport, but a pastime requiring little, if any, athletic skill.

Thank God for Canada's Dick Pound. The commission's rejections were overturned both times at the executive-board level with the help of Pound, son of a past president of the Montreal Thistle Curling Club. Pound, at that time the first vice-president of the IOC, defended curling and was able to force the file back to the program commission for further study.

But it was the same story a year later. The program commission once again slammed the door in curling's face. One of the most influential voices against curling was Canadian ski great Ken Read, the athletes' representative

on the commission. Read was brutally blunt in his assessment of curling: "I am there to express my opinion, not follow some party line," Read said. "There are too many 'paper federations' on the WCF list of members. Curling may be ready by 2002 or 2006, but I feel strongly that it does not yet meet the 'widely practised' requirements of the IOC."

Read's comments were like a kick to the stomach. No one understood why he was launching such a personal attack against a sport that was so strong in his native land, except perhaps to strengthen his own position on the commission. Who knows? Who cares? All that mattered was that curling hit a roadblock one more time. To make matters worse, women's ice hockey,

The 1998 Winter Olympics gold medalists from Switzerland: Dominic Andres, Diego Perren, Daniel Muller, Patrik Loertscher, and Patrick Hurliman.

53

with twenty participating countries and only two world championships behind it, was recommended for inclusion, starting in 1998.

Still, there was no quitting in curling's ruling body. Some of that backroom lobbying I mentioned earlier now swung into high gear as Pound and Hummelt made last-minute pleas to the appropriate IOC people. We even got help from the Japanese, who pleaded directly to IOC president Juan Antonio Samaranch to include curling as part of the medal program for the 1998 Olympics in Nagano.

Everything that could be done was done. Now all we could do was wait.

All the hard work was about to pay off. Curling was granted full-medal status for the year 2002, but, as everybody knows, we were included in the 1998 Nagano Games after the Japanese provided a curling facility.

I found out about curling's acceptance in the most innocent manner. I was reading the paper one Saturday morning in July near my Vancouver home when an article in the sports section caught my eye. My eyes bugged out when I read the story. Curling was in, and not as a demo sport this time. At last, after all the agonies, all the years of waiting, all the failures and the frustrations, curling was back in the Olympics. This was unbelievable!

My first thoughts were of Kingsmith and how proud he would be of what had finally been accomplished from our humble beginnings. Make no mistake, though, he was the guy who got the movement going, and a big reason why curling is in the Olympics today.

Rest easy, old friend.

The Players

Ernie Richardson

You expect your legends to be whiz-bangs at their sports at an early age, like Wayne Gretzky and Tiger Woods. Both were sensational as child protégés.

That wasn't the case with Ernie Richardson. In fact, he was a flop first time out of the hack. He still remembers his first experience in curling with a hint of disgust. "I had tears in my eyes after the game," Richardson said years later. "I was never so discouraged in my life."

Richardson threw his first piece of granite in 1944 as a thirteen-year-old schoolboy substituting in a bonspiel in the little prairie town of Stoughton, Saskatchewan. It was a terrible introduction to the sport. The natural ice was so heavy that young Ernie failed to get a single rock to the house. The game, for the moment, had beaten him. He viewed curling as "that lousy game" and went on to other sports. But curling would not see the last of Richardson. And thank goodness for that.

People who watched him, or had the pleasure of playing against him, often call Richardson the game's consummate player. Debates of this sort, of course, are never wholly satisfactory—no one is entirely convinced one way or the other, because so much rests on subjective analysis. But there is no question the close-knit Richardson clan was the best team of its era, and Big Ern was its leader. He shepherded the team to four Brier titles in a span of five years, and so dominated the game that sometimes it seemed no other teams existed.

The Richardson clan burst on the scene in 1959 at the Brier in Quebec City. Not much was known about the sodbusters from Regina except the quaint fact that they were all related. Richardson's brother Sam played second, and cousins Arnold and Wes held down the third and lead positions (Wes was replaced by Mel Perry in 1963). They weren't expected to win. But they did in spectacular style. Richardson rolled to a 9-1 record and drubbed Edmonton's Herb Olson 12-6 in a sudden-death playoff for the championship.

Richardson would go on to win the Brier again in 1960, 1962, and 1963, meanwhile creating a mystique that lingers today. The strange part is, the legend has distorted the actual portrait. Richardson became known as "The King" and, although there was a regal air about him on and off the ice, he was really a down-to-earth guy. He liked a good party just like anybody else.

Sam recalls the 1963 Brandon Brier, where the partying kept going non-stop and Ernie would enjoy every minute of it.

"Somebody always had a key to our room," he said, "and when we'd come back from the arena there were always about forty Saskatchewan people in our room having a party, telling us they had bet money on us. Ernie would tell them, if they let us get to bed, maybe we'd win it for them."

Ernie loved everything about the game, including its traditions. He especially loved marching behind the bagpipes. Perhaps that's why he played so well in the Scotch Cup. The pipes were going all the time.

The Scotch Cup began as a challenge match between Canada and Scotland in 1959 and was billed as the world championship. The Richardsons, the Brier champs, represented Canada and completely befuddled the Scots that first year. The Canadians had long slides, swept with corn brooms, and played a strong hitting game. The Scots, skipped by Willie Young, released their stones before the front circle, swept with brushes, and played a draw game. Ernie played a game unfamiliar to the Scots. He would have the front end peel guards, or throw rocks deliberately through the house to protect a lead, strategies that infuriated some Scottish fans. "That's nae curling!" they would scream. The Richardsons played in four Scotch Cup competitions and won them all.

One of the reasons for the team's success was bloodlines. They knew each other so well. Sam tells this story of a Canadian championship when Ernie asked him what the ice was like. "Yorkton," he said. "Second end." Ernie knew exactly what he meant. Yorkton is where the Richardson boys had won the provincial title that year.

Of course, there was another reason for the team's great success. "We had the best skip," Sam says flatly.

Richardson, who retired from curling shortly after his heyday, admits he had a wonderful run in the sport. His four Brier victories are still unmatched.

"When you win four, they're all sort of your favorites," Ernie says. "And it's hard not to have the fourth one stick out because that was the record. That was the most rewarding one. But the toughest one was in Kitchener in 1962. We were fortunate."

Richardson ended up in a three-way tie for first place with Alberta's Hec Gervais and Norm Houck's Manitoba foursome. They drew peas to see who got the bye to the final. Big Ern, as usual, got the edge. "I said to Hec—and it really bugged him—that we should have got the bye anyway because we'd beaten him and Houck in the round-robin."

Gervais knocked off Houck in the playoff in a titanic struggle, and it was

Opposite: Ernie Richardson at the 1962 world curling championships in Scotland.

Only three curlers have ever won four world championship titles. From the left, Ernie Richardson, Arnold Richardson, and Garnet (Sam) Richardson, who won the title in 1959, 1960, 1962, 1963. The fourth player in the photo, Wes Richardson, was part of the championship team in 1959, 1960, 1962.

Richardson and Gervais for all the marbles. It was another of the great battles between the two great teams in the 1960s. Richardson's team was outstanding. "We made our first forty-seven shots," Ernie would say several years later. "I was told that by a Regina announcer who was broadcasting the game. We were ahead 7-2. We had to finish the twelve ends in those days and we had it won going into the twelfth so we decided to get all sixteen rocks in the house in the last end. Got fifteen of 'em in there, too."

The Richardsons went their different ways in 1964 and remain scattered today. Ernie, sixty-seven, and the owner of the Richardson House of Fixtures and Supplies lighting company, lives in Regina half the year. He also has a home in Scottsdale, Arizona.

Ernie had a bearing, class, and stature all his own, but he was never ego-driven, and today remains uncomfortable with the idea he's one of the greatest curlers who ever lived. "I've never heard Ernie tell anybody he was a great curler or rich," Sam says. "And he was both."

Hector Gervais

He was called "The Friendly Giant," and for good reason. Hector Gervais was a mountain of a man. He weighed more than 270 pounds (125 kg) throughout most of his curling career, but that didn't stop him from being one of the game's great players. He had the touch of a butterfly when it came to drawing the four-foot circle. That touch carried Gervais to Brier titles in 1961 and 1974, and, more importantly, into the hearts of Canadians who warmed to his gentle humor and down-home charm.

Most people got to watch Hector's magnificent abilities from a distance. I was one of the lucky ones. I played front end for Hector in 1974, and it will always be the greatest curling season of my life.

Gervais was a potato and chicken farmer who, as a teenager, wanted to be a professional football lineman. Nobody would have picked this mammoth of a man from St. Albert, Alberta, as a future championship curler—especially not in 1953, the year the Edmonton Eskimos coach Darrell Royal put the kibosh on Gervais's gridiron dreams after three Canadian Football League exhibition games.

But Gervais was big enough, heavy enough, and strong enough to be a great football player. But his forte was brains, not brawn. So he gravitated to another sport he loved—curling.

His nickname in the early years was "Tiny." Later, they called him the Friendly Giant, although he wasn't always good-humored. "I wasn't that friendly on the ice," he recalled a few months prior to his death. "I had to concentrate when I played. If I was ahead in the game, I could be more friendly."

Gervais showed early he had the goods to be a great player. He could make all the shots and had keen insights on how games were won. The great Matt Baldwin noticed him and, after watching Hector win his third Edmonton bonspiel in a row, invited him to join his team. Baldwin, who won the Brier three times, often says his 1960 team with Gervais was his best ever, even though it never got out of the province. Hector, however, was born to skip, and the union was over after one season. The brilliant career of Hector Gervais was about to take off.

The following season Gervais went back to skipping and, with nineteen-year-old Ron Anton at third, led his team to the 1961 Brier championship in Calgary, losing only one game along the way. A few weeks later, in Scotland, Gervais was world champion after winning the Scotch Cup.

It was the golden era for curling, especially on the Canadian prairies, where the best teams in the world were continually knocking heads. And two of the best happened to be Gervais and Ernie Richardson's clan from Regina. The two teams had one of the game's fiercest rivalries going, but no game they played was bigger than the sudden-death playoff for the 1962 Brier title in Kitchener. Richardson won it, ending a three-way playoff that also included Manitoba's Norm Houck.

Gervais was back in the Brier in 1970, where he again ran smack into one of the era's great teams. Don Duguid of Manitoba finished 9-1 to win the Brier in his home town of Winnipeg, but Gervais was right behind in second.

The big guy struggled after that. His immense weight and years looked like they might be catching up to him. Some people close to the game thought he was through. Then along came that magical year when he captured lightning in a bottle, and I was along for the ride.

Gervais was wonderful to play for because he was so focused. I will always remember the first day of the 1974 city playdowns in Edmonton. We were playing on an outside sheet of ice and, for a moment, second Darrel Sutton and I were standing at the hog line watching play on an adjacent sheet. Then we heard that booming voice from behind our sheet. "Hey, you

Hector Gervais delivers at the 1974 world curling championship in Bern, Switzerland.

guys, we're playing on this sheet of ice." Gervais had been pretty passive for several weeks, but it seemed he was back in the game.

For the next month the man was brilliant, making shot after shot, as we marched inexorably to the Brier title. In some way his performance defied all logic. He delivered the stone in a totally unorthodox manner and often called impossible shots. But he made them. No one was more competitive or demanding of his team. He asked only that we have faith and never question what he was doing.

Still, he was a man of good humor and quick wit, and always liked to make jokes about his teammates. He would often kid that curling would be a lot more fun if he had three robots to play with. Competitors loved being around Gervais. He would often play them in a big game in a bonspiel, then join them for cards after the draw.

"He always played to win—he would be all over his own players on the ice if they swept a rock wrong," three-time world champion Ron Northcott recalls. "But Hector had total respect, and he was popular with all the curlers and fans. Because of his size and touch, everybody liked to watch him play."

Gervais died of a massive heart attack at the age of sixty-three on July 19, 1997. He had been plagued with a heart problem for almost two decades and had undergone heart surgery in 1987. His passing was a great loss to curling. I'll never forget him, or that wonderful season in 1974.

Vera Pezer

Long before Sandra Schmirler was kicking the stuffing out of everybody on a curling sheet, there was another Saskatchewan women's "super" team. In a way, Saskatoon's Vera Pezer played lead for Schmirler, who has skipped the most dominant women's team in the 1990s.

"I really think we were the prototype of what they [Schmirler] are now," says Pezer, looking back thirty years to her own remarkable career in the sport. "Her team reminds me of our team a lot: people working as a unit, as a team."

Pezer's era started in 1969, when she won her first Canadian championship as third for Joyce McKee, the first big name in the history of women's curling. Two seasons later, the team—by this time greatly reconfigured—returned to the national scene. Pezer was now skip, with Sheila Rowan at third, McKee at second, and Lenore Morrison at lead. The changes helped as the foursome swept the next three Canadian championships. They never got a chance to pursue a world title, because there was no such event at the time, but there's little doubt the Saskatchewan women would have dominated that, too.

Vera Pezer led the team that won the 1971 championship in St. John's and the 1973 championship in Charlottetown. From the left: Vera Pezer, Sheila Rowan, Joyce McKee, and Lenore Morrison

It was a sensational three-year run of curling and stamped Pezer as one of the greatest women curlers of all time.

The Vera Pezer story began in a rural setting. Meskanaw is not much different from most Saskatchewan hamlets. During Pezer's youth there were two stores, three grain elevators, a garage, a café, a hotel, and, of course, a curling rink.

The strongest influence in her life was her dad. He was a curler and the caretaker of the two-sheet, natural-ice rink. After supper she would trundle along with him and play on one sheet while he worked on the other. "It was a time we shared together," Pezer says.

The effect of all that throwing made young Vera a good shotmaker, but she was denied a chance to play on a team and compete in the high-school bonspiel because of her age. It only made her hungrier. After high school she moved to Saskatoon, where she received the proper coaching in university and learned the slide better.

"I eventually reached a point where I was mature enough to handle the pressure," says Pezer. "In the 1970s I reached my peak."

The 1972 Canadian title was special for Pezer because it was the first Macdonald Lassie and was played in front of friends and family in Saskatoon. "We lost our first game to Quebec, but from then on it was the best week we ever put together," she says. "The third one (1973) was significant because no one had won three in a row."

It was a different time and a different era. Curlers played the game for fun and didn't get caught up in what they were doing. It took Pezer a long time to finally look back and realize what she and her teammates had accomplished.

"During those five years, you didn't think about it; you just kept going one year at a time. It wasn't until ten years later that I could look back and say, 'Hey, that was really something.' But it was a wonderful time to be a curler, and a wonderful time to be winning."

Incredibly, the team broke up right after its third straight Canadian championship. In fact, it wasn't long after that Pezer stopped playing the game altogether to seek a doctorate in psychology. "I quit partly because I'd burned out," says Pezer, who kept in touch with the game by becoming a sports psychologist and working for a time with Curl Canada. "Your priorities change over time. Other things become more important."

Pezer eventually came back to the game she loved and, through her profession, came to help other curlers deal with the mental side of the game. Pezer even got to know Schmirler and members of her team in the late 1980s and offered them some advice.

"What I like," says Pezer, "is that the two most successful women's teams in Canadian curling history come from Saskatchewan. That's something our team and their team should be proud of."

The greatest female curler in the history of the sport was Joyce McKee of Saskatoon, Saskatchewan. McKee won the Canadian women's curling championship a record five times, two as skip and three at second. McKee (far right) is shown here with the 1992 Seniors championship team of Sheila Rowan, Donna Trapp, and Doreen Thomas. Rowan was part of three Canadian women's championship teams that McKee was part of (1971, 1972, 1973).

Joyce McKee

Diminutive Joyce McKee of Saskatoon has always been breaking new ground in women's curling. McKee was the first woman to skip her team to two Canadian championships, and she still leads women with five national titles, the last three as second for Vera Pezer.

Her need to show the way began in 1951 when, as an eighteen-year-old player, she made local history by playing in the tough Saskatoon men's league with her father, Hugh McKee. The foursome traveled 26 miles (42 km) from their homes in Asquith to play in the league, and young Joyce was the only female. Her presence caused something of an uproar because, for one thing, the young woman was outplaying most of the men. Enough of that! The league closed the loophole, and the following year the league was all-male and McKee was back in women's curling.

But the experience did wonders for her confidence. She also developed a style and strategy that would carry her to the top of women's curling in Canada.

McKee's strengths were her fierce competitiveness and a silky-smooth delivery that became her trademark. The delivery came a long way over the years, because her first attempts at the sport were less than inspiring. McKee remembers her first game in Asquith, where she was entered in a high-school bonspiel at the age of fifteen. "I only weighed 75 pounds [34 kg]," she says, "and I had to put both feet in the hack and both hands on the stone in order to get it down the ice."

She loved the game immediately and was determined to be better. It helped that McKee was a natural athlete, especially in softball. She honed her game in those early years and, before long, was dominating women's curling in Saskatoon. She ran up a remarkable string of victories in the Saskatoon bonspiel. In a nine-year period between 1953 and 1961, McKee went 82-9, and on three occasions went through the bonspiel unbeaten.

McKee was a pioneer in the sport. When she arrived on the scene, the Macdonald Brier was an institution in men's curling, but there was nothing for the women except their own provincial championships. But all that was about to change. McKee won the Western Canadian championship in 1960, then traveled east to Oshawa to compete in an exhibition series against teams from Ontario and Quebec. McKee was sensational and won handily.

The following year the first official Canadian women's championship, sponsored by Dominion Stores, was held in Ottawa, and McKee's team sailed through the nine-team competition without a loss. Along the way she faced Toronto's Emily Wooley, considered the best team in the east at the time. McKee won 10-4, and Wooley was stunned by the play of the Saskatoon outfit. Wooley, sixty-seven at the time, called McKee the finest player she had played in a lifetime of curling.

McKee won her second national title as a skip in 1969 in Thunder Bay, then turned the skipping reins over to Vera Pezer. Together they would win three more national titles, and McKee would emerge a curling legend in the country.

Don Duguid

Tension crackled like an electric charge. The 1970 Brier was drawing to a climax, and in the thick of the drama was Don Duguid. The little guy with the big shots had the Brier title within his grasp in front of his hometown fans in Winnipeg. One shot to win and Duguid, hunkered in the hack, had to throw it. Up in the stands, 10,000 fans in the Winnipeg Arena held their collective breath.

"It had been so loud in the Winnipeg Arena all week, but ours was the last game to finish on that draw," Duguid recalled. "And when I went to throw my last shot, the whole place just went so quiet. I found that a little unnerving."

If there was a defining moment in Duguid's glittering curling career, this was it. Dugie, who had never lacked for confidence in his abilities on a sheet of ice, was thrown the ultimate challenge for a skip. Did he have what it takes? Now he was face-to-face with the answer.

In a few moments a legend was born to the sound of a tremendous roar. In a thunderclash finish, Duguid picked out an enemy stone belonging to Saskatchewan's Bob (Peewee) Pickering to secure the win and the Brier title. Duguid came in an economy-sized package, but, as he demonstrated that March day in Winnipeg, he was a big man under pressure.

The 1970 Brier victory was just the start of big things for "The Digit" and his crack team from the Granite Club, which included third Rod (The Arrow) Hunter, Jim Pettapiece, and Bryan Wood. They went on to win the world championship, and then repeated the whole process the following year with Brier and world titles.

Duguid had a wonderful team—"a perfect fit," he would often say. Hunter threw laser beams, and the front end was one of the best sweeping units ever

Don Duguid delivers at the 1970 world curling championship in Utica, New York. Duguid won that title and another one year later in Megere, France.

put together. But Dugie was the leader. There was no question who the boss was when the team stepped on the ice. Strategy conferences were few. Dugie put the broom down and that was it—end of discussion. And he backed up his unshakable confidence with his superb shotmaking ability.

Duguid had been building toward his time in the spotlight since he was a kid. He learned to curl by sneaking into the Victoria Curling Club in Winnipeg, where his father worked as an icemaker, in the wee small hours of the morning.

"We'd wait until we heard pop coming in after locking up for the night," he remembered. "Then we'd slip out the back door, squeeze through a bend in the barred windows, and throw rocks in the dark. We'd open the shutters over sheet five for a little light. We lived just around the corner, but Pop couldn't see from the house. Later I took over as icemaker and cleaner-upper on weekends."

It was the game's golden age. It was a time in Winnipeg that curling stars such as Jimmy Welsh, Howard Wood, and Ken Watson were no less famous than hockey players in the NHL. Young curlers like Duguid could rub shoulders with the best in the world without leaving home.

Duguid loved being around his "heroes," and he especially loved the game. It was only a matter of time until he started to have some success of his own. He appeared in his first Brier in 1957 as second for Manitoba's Howard Wood Jr. They didn't win that year, but Dugie had a taste of the big time and he liked it. He moved up to third and helped Terry Braunstein win the Brier in 1965. That was the high. The low came a few weeks later when the Canadians crashed and burned at the Scotch Cup, losing to Bud Somerville of the United States in the final. It was the first Canadian team to lose the international title, and Duguid says it left an empty feeling in his stomach.

He made up for it, though, with his back-to-back world titles at the Silver Broom in 1970–71. His team never lost a game, sweeping all seventeen matches. Try doing that sometime.

Duguid retired at the top of his game at age thirty-four. Shortly after winning his second world title, he walked away from competitive curling to take on the challenging role of color commentator with the CBC. He sometimes looks back and wonders what he left on the table when he gave up the game. "The only regret I have is that, had we stuck together, we might have been the first to win three in a row, maybe even four, because that team was that good."

Dugie has since become a household name in Canada after years in the broadcast booth, where he hasn't been afraid to dish out his opinions.

"Dugie is a character on television," says Hugh Carruthers, who was a long-time producer of CBC Curling on *Sportsweekend*. "I call him Dizzy Duguid because he reminds me a lot of Dizzy Dean, that great baseball announcer. Dean slaughtered the language, but people loved him. They used to get letters from teachers about Dugie. They've stopped writing. They gave up. I wouldn't change Dugie for a minute. He just adds so much."

Here, Matt Baldwin, second from the right, is pictured with Pat Ryan (world champion in 1984, 1994), Hector Gervais Jr., and Kevin Martin (Brier champion in 1991, 1997). The four were part of the ceremonial rock team at the 1999 Labatt Brier in Edmonton.

Matt Baldwin

Curling has had its share of characters down through the years. But it's doubtful there will ever be another Matt Baldwin. He was curling's first supreme showman who helped kick-start curling in northern Alberta during the postwar boom, inspiring a whole new era of enthusiasm for the game.

Baldwin took up curling in a period when it was still considered "an old man's game." Skips were typically fifty or sixty years old. But it was a time of transition, and Baldwin was the man to help move the game forward. "I figured it was a hell of a sport," Baldwin recalls. "Four guys can get together and drink, play cards, and have a great time. I figured it was too good for the old guys."

Fun: That was Baldwin's first commandment in curling, and he lived it to the hilt during a sparkling career. He won the Brier in 1954, 1957, and 1958, and was in two others, in 1956 and 1971. He is one of only four men to skip at least three Brier winners, and one of seven to post back-to-back wins. That's pretty heady stuff, and yet when people talk about Baldwin, they talk about the character first.

He was always the good-humor man. If he felt tired or was feeling the rigors of the night before, he brought a chair with him and sat down between shots. When the lights went out in Quebec City during the 1971 Brier, the opposing skip was horrified to find Baldwin had scored an eight-ender in the pitch-dark arena by arranging the stones. It was vintage Baldwin, who had done the dirty deed between trips to the blacked-out bar.

Baldwin says he loved the game the minute he played it. But the Brier was what lured him. "From the time I was a kid in Saskatchewan—I was conscripted to curl when I was fourteen because, back in 1940, everybody else was at war—the Brier was the ultimate," he admitted. "Just to get there would have been something. I should have paid more attention to my studies when I was in university than I did. I came damn close to screwing it up, simply because of curling. I was addicted to it. I always thought if I could win the Brier, that would be better than getting a degree."

Baldwin's passion for the game drove him, and he made his first appearance in a Brier at home. The 1954 Brier was held in the Edmonton Gardens, and with Baldwin in the field, it was a smash hit. The Brier drew 32,000 spectators that year, considered a phenomenal figure at the time. After that, curling in the area boomed. "It was a big to do," Baldwin would say later. "Within the next two or three years, our rink [Glenn Gray, Pete Ferry, and Jim Collins] must have opened ten to twelve new curling rinks. Curling was just starting to take off at that point."

Baldwin's victory at the 1954 Brier wasn't the only story that year. There was "The Slide." If curlers thought the great Manitoba skip Ken Watson had a long slide, they hadn't seen anything until they'd seen Baldwin. Responding to the spectators' requests, he demonstrated his ability to slide in the final game of the round-robin championship.

"I was in a very euphoric mood, knowing I had won it," said Baldwin, "and, being a semi-showoff, I wound up with as hard of a push as I could have managed and got halfway down the sheet. I had people tell me since then I went all the way down the ice, but that's not the truth. Anyway, I just about came to a stop and gave the rock a shove and, wouldn't you know it, it ended up right on the button." The crowd went nuts and a legend was born.

Baldwin would reenact the slide many times over his career. He would (in jest) slide the entire length of the ice and drop a 40-pound (18-kg) stone on the button, slowly making a complete circle with his body, and tip his peaked cap to the delight of other curlers and the crowd.

Baldwin remembers experimenting with the slide delivery along with Gray after completing his university degree in petroleum engineering in 1951. While Watson had been sliding to the front of the house for years, most curlers barely got 4 feet (120 cm) out of the hack at the time. Baldwin called it a "fluke" when he discovered he could slide farther than anyone else wearing a pair of Oxford shoes that he had resoled. He maintained the advantage until Teflon was invented in the early 1960s.

"This hunk of leather was the hardest thing I'd ever seen in my life," he would say. "I mean you could hardly cut it with a knife. I kept wetting it and letting it dry out and sliding on it, and this thing got to be very slippery. And the more I used it, the tougher and harder it got, and the more it would slide." By the time he won the first of his three Briers, Baldwin could easily reach the hog line. "It wasn't in the rules at that point," he says. "You could go as far as you wanted." Eventually a rule was put in place calling for rocks to be released before crossing the hog line.

Baldwin spends most of his time today in Indian Wells, California, enjoying semi-retirement after a career as owner of several successful oil-patch servicing companies. He no longer curls but still holds the game close to his heart. "My hair still stands on end when I hear the bagpipes," he says.

Paul Gowsell

If curling ever needed a player to shake it up, he was found in Calgary in the mid-1970s. Paul Gowsell, a young man with flaming red hair and a temperament to match, bewitched, bothered, and bewildered the custodians of the game's mores for five tumultuous years. The game had been orderly, sensible, and, above all, courteous. Then along came Gowsell, exploding our myths and, all the time, yapping, yapping, yapping.

Beneath the exterior lie tales of pizza delivered on the ice, wild parties, and running battles with curling officials. But they would mean nothing without Gowsell's ability to throw stones and play the game. He never won a Brier. His one and only appearance was in 1980 in Calgary. But he was an outstanding curler who engraved his own spirit into the pop culture of Canadian sport.

Gowsell's career was like a comet racing across the sky. He blazed across, and then he was gone. He was virtually unstoppable from 1976 to 1980, winning two world junior championships, an Alberta men's title, and more money than at any time in the game's history. He seemed poised for a long and riotous career on the pebbled ice. Then, just like that, he was gone, for reasons nobody quite understands. But while he played he was on all the seismic scales and the biggest name in the sport.

He was his own man on the ice and off. If curling officials didn't like his style, the hell with them, he would say. He would bang his broom, berate his own teammates, and often stare down his opponents, who didn't always know what to make of him. Gowsell would say it was all part of his tactics to be the best player he could be.

Gowsell loved a party. The night after his first Canadian junior men's victory in 1976, Gowsell grabbed the mike at the celebration at Edmonton's Doone High School and invited the whole dance back to his hotel for a drink. Three hundred kids showed up. So did the police to throw them all out. The newspapers loved it, and Gowsell's career as an "enfant terrible" had begun.

But that was nothing. Gowsell came to the public's attention in a big way while winning his first world junior championship in Scotland later that year with Neil Houston, Glen Jackson, and Kelly Stearne. The Calgary curlers got into a big row over charges that they were sweeping improperly, and stories of Gowsell's international dust-up with officials carried all the way back to Canada. Gowsell refused to apologize for his behavior. This was war, he said, and through the rest of his days in the curling spotlight it was one battle after another.

Paul Gowsell skipped his Canadian foursome to the world junior title in 1976 and again in 1978. No other curler in the world has equaled his feat.

Gowsell never minded the press running with stories of his partying, carousing, or bickering. "It doesn't bother me," he would say, "as long as they're accurate." The more the press paid attention, the more Gowsell would talk. He rarely turned down interviews, which made him a media darling.

But more than anything, Gowsell was a winner. His team won $70,000 in 1978, another $70,000 in 1979, and $40,000 in 1980, numbers that boggled the imagination at the time. If there was cash on the table, Gowsell usually won it. It meant two things: he could continue to party and not worry about having to find a job. "I took a lot of pride in not having to work," he would say. "I liked the party life; it was a lot of fun."

But winning was no fluke. The team practiced a lot and played with a feeling of invincibility. Gowsell was capable of making some of the most fantastic shots imaginable. He had a keen sense of what it took to win, and his strategy was often flawless for one so young.

Undoubtedly most of Gowsell's stories will be forgotten long before people stop talking about "The Pizza." At a big bonspiel in Saskatoon, Gowsell had the temerity to order a pizza and have it delivered on the ice as the game went on. The spectators were in stitches as Gowsell and his buddies munched on their dinner. "Want some?" Gowsell asked opponent Larry McGrath.

Gowsell has never managed to recapture his glory years. The 1980 Brier was his last showcase event. His teams gradually broke up and he eventually entered the mainstream. He got a job, got married, and started a family. He had some mild success with other line-ups, but it was never the same.

But then again, how could it be?

Bud Somerville

In many respects, Bud Somerville stands out as one of the most remarkable curlers who ever lived. Just consider, as a starter, these two facts. He represented the United States, where the sport has never really flourished on a grand scale. Then there was his health. He suffered serious heart problems during his career that almost cost him his life.

Still, Somerville overcame the obstacles to become the best player ever produced in the United States, and one of the finest in the history of the game. Today, he is a curling legend in his own country and around the world.

Somerville made his place in history early. He took a decidedly underdog U.S. team and shocked everybody—including himself—by winning the 1965 world championship. His win broke Canada's six-year stranglehold on the Scotch Cup championship and brought into focus Somerville's curling abilities.

"I didn't expect it [to win]," Somerville remembers. "When you go to those things, you expect everyone else to be a lot better than you, but we all have to throw the stones and anything can happen."

Bud Somerville has played in the world curling championship a total of six times, returning as the champion in 1965 and again in 1974. He is shown here delivering at the 1969 championship in Perth, Scotland.

His win had a huge impact on the game at the time. It proved that Canadians were not invincible supermen on the ice, and that other countries could play the game at a high level. Somerville, though, had to suffer some slings and arrows from his Canadian counterparts, who were not too happy to see someone else climb onto the world podium.

"It was pretty popular in every place other than Canada," Somerville says. "I think the Europeans felt it was good for the sport of curling."

It was also the beginning of a glorious career for Somerville, whose résumé is festooned with titles and honors. He skipped teams to fourteen state, five national, and two world titles (the other came in 1974). His drive and determination were unmatched. He came back from open-heart surgery in 1988 to compete on the U.S. Olympic team when curling debuted as a demonstration sport. The Americans finished second. He also played in the 1992 Olympics, and was fifth man on his son's world team in 1994. It's not surprising that Somerville was the first inductee into the U.S. Curling Hall of Fame.

Somerville says there's no great secret behind his success. He loved the game, hated to lose, and didn't mind practicing to get better.

"I've never been a good loser," he says, "even when I was a kid. I didn't like losing at cards, checkers, or whatever. So I worked hard at it. I'd go down to the club and throw rocks all day."

His introduction to the game was typical for most kids in the 1940s. Somerville's parents would bring him down to the local club in Superior, Wisconsin, when he was nine years old. "I'd watch my dad curl, but I liked monkeying around on the ice better than actually watching the game," says Somerville. "He'd take me out and push me on a rock. Then I started skipping in high school, and played four years with my dad before I skipped my own team."

Somerville introduced his son to the game in much the same way. Today, Tim Somerville is one of the best skips in the United States. But he'll have to go a long way to match the brilliant career of his father, who helped put the United States on the world curling map.

Ken Watson

Turn back the clock half a century or more and try to visualize the game of curling. Our curler is an older man, perhaps in his fifties or sixties, and the game is dull, uninspiring, and not played with much imagination or skill. That is certainly not the way the game looks today. Curling has gone up-tempo. It is played at a high level by young curlers of both sexes who are well schooled in the game's fundamentals.

Thank you, Ken Watson.

It's difficult to single out one individual who revolutionized any sport, but there can be no doubt Watson, in many ways, changed the face of curling. He popularized the game across the country in the 1940s and 1950s, and helped move it along to where it is today—an international sport worthy of the Olympic Games.

Watson was a marvelous player during his career in Winnipeg. He skipped the 1936, 1942, and 1949 Brier winners, losing only a total of two games along the way. He won the grand aggregate in the mammoth Manitoba Bonspiel in 1939, then reeled off six more in a row between 1942 and 1947. He was undoubtedly the finest curler of his time, and an argument can be made that he was the greatest curler in history.

His ability on the ice was amazing at the time. Watson was so good he could also win with almost anybody. His only constant was at third, where brother Grant was a fixture. But each time he went to the Brier, he had a different front end. In 1936, it was Marvin MacIntyre and Charlie Kerr; in 1942, Charlie Scrymgeour and Jim Grant; seven years later, in 1949, he had Lyle Dyker and Charlie Reid.

Watson was way ahead of his time, and put his biggest imprint on the game with the development of the long slide. His graceful delivery moved the Brier into national prominence and captured the imagination of a whole new breed of curler.

He was a great curler but an even better student of the game. He especially liked the great Gordon Hudson, and watched him at every opportunity, trying to duplicate his mannerisms. But he couldn't duplicate his slide. Then, late one night, he discovered that sliding came easier when he removed his toe rubber from the front foot and slid on the sole of the leather shoe. He discovered he could slide even further than Hudson. Watson and his friends worked on the sliding delivery for the next few years and, by the early 1930s, had perfected it.

The sliding delivery created a great deal of controversy. Older curlers felt it gave young whippersnappers like Watson an unfair advantage because they were closer to the target on release. But the genie was out of the bottle. "The Winnipeg Slide," as it came to be known, was athletically demanding but also esthetically pleasing, and all young curlers wanted to adopt it. Soon young men everywhere were sliding out to the hog line.

Watson's contributions to the game go far, far beyond the ice and Brier victories. He was also a tireless worker on behalf of the sport he loved. One of Watson's great contributions was promoting the game and making it easier for people—especially young people—to play. He wrote instruction columns in newspapers, as well as four books on curling. His book *Ken Watson on Curling*, published in 1950, is a landmark in the sport. It sold more than 150,000 copies and was the bible for every young curler learning the game. It is still in use today. He also produced and directed a film, *Magic in Curling*, which won an award at the Cannes Film Festival in 1956.

He was one of the first big-name curlers to appreciate the importance of attracting kids to curling. He was a native son of Manitoba, born in Minnedosa and educated in Winnipeg public schools. He taught high school for twenty

Ken Watson: three-time Brier champion, curling author, curling administrator, instructor, and student of the game.

years in Winnipeg, and during this time was the man behind the formation of schoolboy curling. When the Brier was held in Victoria in 1958, officials were astounded when they realized the average age of the competitors was under thirty. A few short years before, men in their fifties and sixties had dominated the game.

Watson was also instrumental in helping the Scotch Cup, the forerunner of the world curling championships, get off the ground. He was invited to Scotland in 1959 to meet with advocates of a Canada–Scotland series. He took a lot of heat for that because he was acting on his own, outside the Dominion Curling Association. Canadian officials objected to Canadian curlers becoming too closely associated with a whiskey company. But the series proceeded anyway and became a hit.

Watson is a member of the Canadian Sports Hall of Fame, the Canadian Curling Hall of Fame, and the Manitoba Sports Hall of Fame. In 1978, he was the inaugural recipient of the Elmer Freytag Memorial Award for his contribution in establishing the world curling championship.

Bernie Sparkes

When you open the curling record books, there is one name that stands out from all of the rest—Bernie Sparkes. He has earned this distinction because he has played in a total of twelve Briers, two more than any other curler in Canada. It is a standard that is unlikely to ever be topped.

Sparkes made a name in the sport in his native Alberta. He played second for the great Ron (The Owl) Northcott of Calgary, who won three Canadian and world championships in four trips between 1966 and 1969. During his days in Alberta, Sparkes formed a front-end combination with Fred Storey that, some say, was the best ever. During those years Sparkes was named to the Brier's first all-star team a total of three times.

That would have been enough to get Sparkes into any curling Hall of Fame. But he wasn't through, yet. He moved west to Vancouver, British Columbia, and carved out the second half of his brilliant career as a world-class skip. Even though he never won a national title for his adopted province, Sparkes is still its most celebrated male curler, and so he should be. Eight times, from 1972 to 1987, Sparkes represented B.C. at the Macdonald, and then the Labatt Brier, for the Canadian men's championship.

"Curling has been very, very good to me," says Sparkes, who can be found these days living in the Fraser Valley town of Chilliwack, which is only about 55 miles (90 km) from the bustle of Vancouver, but about a million miles from the glare and notoriety of competitive curling. "I have met a lot of terrific people over the years. Curling has contributed to my income, and added a great deal to my life."

It is ironic how his life has gone full circle for Sparkes. He got interested in curling at a tender age in Claresholm, Alberta, where his father was the

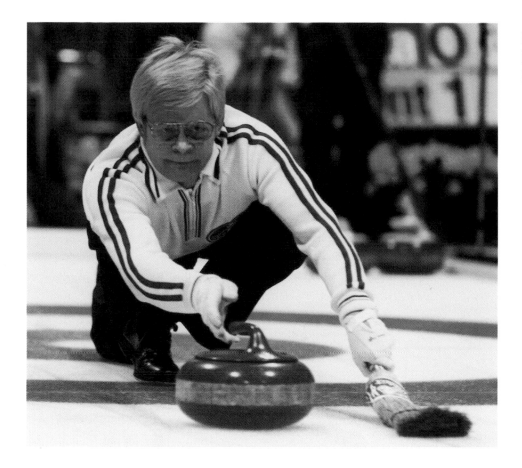

Bernie Sparkes delivers during his last of twelve Brier appearances, in Edmonton in 1987.

icemaker at the local curling club. "I used to throw rocks waiting for him to finish up at night," Sparkes recalls. "I was what was termed a rink-rat. I was there all the time after school and on the weekends."

Sparkes enjoyed a great career, but it wasn't all roses. One Brier that wasn't so good and was a precursor to his retirement to the Fraser Valley was the 1987 rendition in Edmonton, and the manner in which he let it get away from him was particularly unfortunate. He had Ontario's Russ Howard on the ropes in the championship final. A win over Howard would have given the organizing committee back in Vancouver a big boost for the world championship they were preparing for.

Sparkes had jockeyed into a 7-6 lead, playing the tenth and final end, when disaster struck. Nose hits, questionable calls, and crucial misses led to a five-ender by Howard. Sparkes's best skipping shot at a Canadian title was gone, and he would have to go to B.C. Place Stadium and its temporary rink as a spectator instead of as a conquering hero.

"That end will haunt me for the rest of my life," says Sparkes. "That's the one I almost have nightmares over. I think about what we could have done differently, should have done differently. I felt like I was letting down all those guys who had worked so hard to make sure the world championships were a success."

Sparkes still plays in the men's league once a week at the Chilliwack club. "I just got three other guys and tried to have some fun," he says. "The key word there is 'try' because the competitive juices that flow don't just dry up. It's frustrating because the expectations are a lot higher than my ability to make some of the shots I try to make now."

Ron Northcott

Ron Northcott never invented the Free Guard Zone (FGZ) rule. It only appears that way. The Calgary legend, who won three Canadian and world championships in a glittering career, skipped the style of game we are familiar with today, only he was playing it long before the FGZ was brought in.

    The difference today? Curling needs the FGZ in order to resurrect the kind of excitement the game produced when the bespectacled Northcott and his peers of the 1960s held forth on the Brier and world ice lanes.

Ron Northcott won the last of three world championships at Pointe Claire, Quebec, in 1968, the first year Air Canada sponsored the event that was known as the Air Canada Silver Broom. Northcott proudly displays the trophy that was the icon of world curling for the next eighteen years.

"We didn't need that kind of thing, for sure," says Northcott, more popularly known as "The Owl" during his playing days. "It was a different game then. The ice back in the 1960s, and the use of corn brooms, dictated the same kind of game the FGZ dictates on today's far more predictable, far more consistent, ice, with the use of brushes."

Northcott was a master of the come-around game. And he learned it from one of the best. He graduated to the skipping role after numerous seasons in the company of the late Jimmy Shields, a guy widely known as curling's "Little General." A gambler—and mentor—*extraordinaire*.

"Jimmy liked the finesse game, the quiet weight," Northcott says. "He was an advocate of the come-around with the use of the brooms. I didn't invent that strategy. It just stuck with me when I began skipping. It helped that I had the same great sweeping. It was requisite for the kind of game we played."

Northcott won his titles in three of four years (1966, 1968, 1969) with three different vice-skips and what was generally considered the best front-end sweeping tandem—Bernie Sparkes and Fred Storey—of that or any other era. It allowed Northcott to duck behind a guard and turn the heat up on his opponent.

"It's fair to say that not everybody was as aggressive in those days," he admits. "The general mindset still was, get ahead on the scoreboard and then run. But, like the FGZ makes it tougher to defend a lead now, the likelihood of fanning or nosing a peel was much greater back then. It wasn't so easy to protect a three- or four-point lead then. And we played twelve ends, too. Those conditions dictated your style of play. With our teams, the shooters I had, and the brooms I had, I always figured it made more sense to stay on the offense and score points."

Northcott, who long ago retired to the golf course, says he would have loved to have a chance to play on today's ice surfaces.

"Personally, I think it would be fun to play on the ice they're playing on now. It's relatively perfect. Ice technology has come a long way in thirty years. Throwing a rock into the four-foot in the first end shouldn't be nearly as much of a challenge. Can you imagine how much fun it would be to watch a game today if they used the corn brooms?

"It was altogether different in our day. You went out there in the arena, and the first end was always unbelievably heavy, and even the best brooms didn't help that much. The second end was a bit faster, then it would get quicker and quicker until it was lightning keen, and particularly if there were spots where you'd played a lot of rocks."

Northcott took several more cracks at a record-tying fourth Canadian title in the 1970s but never made it past the Alberta final. He lost to Hec Gervais at the last gasp in 1970, to Mel Watchorn in 1973, and to Tommy Reed in 1977. He described his defeat in '77 as a "real spike in the heart."

Long gone were Sparkes and Storey. Northcott had put together a new lineup and, like days or yore, mowed down the opposition to within one victory of heading to another Brier. "We were 6-0 in a triple-knockout and we needed to beat [Reed] once," Northcott recalls. Reed needed three straight victories over the then forty-one-year-old former champ to advance. And that's exactly what he did.

"The guy was phenomenal," says Northcott. "He made unbelievable shots in all three games. I think that's what did me in. I never gave it much of a shot after that."

Ed Lukowich

Curling is a game steeped in tradition and rules. Ed Lukowich was one of the first great curlers who stepped back, took a look at some of them, and went the other way. He was a renegade who challenged the accepted way of doing things.

But he was also a winner. In a career that stretched three decades, Fast Eddy appeared in five Briers out of Alberta, but could easily have been in five more with a break or two. He made the most of his time in the spotlight, winning two Briers and a world championship. He also appeared in the Olympics in 1988, when it was a demonstration sport, in his home town of Calgary.

Lukowich was always a little different. He was, for instance, one of the few curlers who made the jump successfully from the junior ranks to the Brier. Only five players who have been a part of a junior champion team in their younger years went on to win the Brier. "I guess we were ahead of our time," says Lukowich, who played third for brother Mike in the 1961 and 1962 national schoolboys out of tiny Speers, Saskatchewan, sweeping the competition in 1962 with a 10-0 record. "We would have given anything to have played in a World Junior in those days."

Lukowich quickly earned a reputation as a wonderful shotmaker after graduating to the men's ranks. After a couple of failures at the Alberta provincials, Lukowich and Calgary's Mike Chernoff teamed up in 1978 out of Medicine Hat. Lukowich started the season skipping, but at one point the team hit a tremendous losing streak. The solution was to revamp the roles of skip and third. Lukowich would still throw skip stones, but Chernoff would plot strategy. Critics said the move would never work. It did, immediately, and the Albertans went on to win the Brier, only to lose the world championship later that year.

His world championship finally came in 1986. "It was really pleasing. It was redemption. It was the strongest team I ever curled with," Lukowich says. The Calgary outfit—John Ferguson, Neil Houston, and Brent Syme—earned a bye into the Brier final and beat Ontario's Russ Howard 4-3 in a thriller. A few weeks later in Toronto, Lukowich "struggled for the first time all season" but still came away with the world championship. "The finesse game had been our strength that year, but it didn't work in Toronto," he

says. "The ice was streaky and there were different weight spots. There were some scary moments that week. But, then, it wouldn't be normal if there wasn't in that kind of curling."

Lukowich appeared in his fifth Brier in 1994. Again, he caused heads to turn and tongues to wag. He had taken control of a team in playoff contention after his own squad had been eliminated at the zone level. "Curling is hung up on a lot of traditions and rules that are out of sync with the time," Lukowich would say later. "I guess a lot of people don't share that view."

Curling has always been more than a sport to Lukowich—in many ways it has been his life. He has been the inspiration behind the World Curling Tour, written three books on the sport, made a sixty-minute instructional video, and has nurtured a curling mail-order business. Today Lukowich works as a curling color commentator with CTV Sportsnet.

Ed Lukowich hoists the Macdonald Brier Tankard after winning the coveted trophy in 1978 at the PNE Coliseum in Vancouver.

Sandra Schmirler

There is a natural law in sports by which, ever so often, a new athlete comes around and sets the standard of achievement notably higher than it was ever before. This athlete forces the pace, and the rest have to follow the best they can.

During the last decade we have seen this law at work in curling: Sandra Schmirler has set the bar higher than anyone could imagine. She created one of the great sports dynasties in Canada and, at the same time, turned women's curling into a marketable item. It's no coincidence that the rise in popularity of women's curling on television occurred during the Schmirler years.

And what great years they have been. Schmirler and her Regina teammates, Jan Betker, Joan McCusker, and Marcia Gudereit, dominated Canadian women's curling this decade, winning three national and world championships (1993, 1994, 1997) and an Olympic gold medal (1998). Sweden's Elisabeth Gustafson has since won four women's world titles, but it was Schmirler who set the example for others to follow.

How do you explain such a degree of excellence over a period of time? What makes the team so special? "Obviously we're not going to have success if we're not having fun," Schmirler explains. "Part of the reason we've had huge success is the fact we're having a blast. If you're not having fun, you wouldn't stay together for as long as we have."

But that's only part of it. Much of the team's success has to do with Schmirler. She might be the best big-game player women's curling has ever seen. One of the biggest games came in the Olympic Trials in Brandon in 1997, when Schmirler executed a miraculous angle-raise takeout late in the final that helped her beat Calgary's Shannon Kleibrink. "When the games are most important," Kleibrink says, "Sandra makes the big shots. We outcurled them in the final, but Sandra made one of the best shots under pressure I've ever seen." The facts back her up. Schmirler has been in eight finals at the Scott Tournament of Hearts, World championships, and Olympic Trials and Games. She's won them all.

Schmirler's personality stands out along with her curling exploits. She has a sharp wit and a keen sense of humor. But what makes her great on the ice is her fierce desire to win.

"Sandra's a great player, and she's got the competitive sense," says her husband, Shannon England. "She wants to excel. It's hard for her to go and golf for fun. She wants to do well. She wants to be the best at anything." England tells a story about the first time he went with Schmirler to her parents' home in Biggar, Saskatchewan, where she was raised. "We were playing Ping-Pong when I saw her competitive nature," he explains. "She cleaned my clock, and she was really bugging me. As soon as I beat her, she quit and went upstairs. That's her competitive nature. She wants to win.

Opposite: Sandra Schmirler: Olympic gold medal winner, 1998; women's world champion, 1993, 1994, 1997.

That's all it is—just win, baby. She wants to put effort into anything to win. She works hard at it. She's focused."

Schmirler apparently got her drive to win from her father and her maternal grandmother, Mabel McLeod, who loved to prevail at cribbage. She was active in sports throughout school. In her senior year at Biggar Composite High School, she played senior women's volleyball and badminton.

Her parents, Art and Shirley Schmirler, tell of the time their daughter swam in the provincial meet despite the fact she had cut off the end of a finger less than a week earlier. She won the gold medal by freezing the finger just before the race. "She always did have that competitive spirit," Shirley says. "She had to beat me at whatever she was doing. But she's coachable, too. If a coach said do this, she'd do her utmost to do it."

Schmirler's curling career almost never happened. In high school she had to choose between curling and basketball. She chose curling but wasn't sure about the decision. But her high-school coach, Mel Tryhuba, sensed that Schmirler was a special talent. "All along she was an outstanding shotmaker. I didn't know she would ever be a world champion or be going to the Olympics. I certainly saw she could go far in curling and be a provincial contender if she got together with the right ladies."

The "right" ladies did come along. Third Betker and Schmirler had curled together since 1985. After the 1990 competitive season, they decided to start their own team, with Schmirler as the skip. They phoned several people to join them, finally hearing back from McCusker, who said she would play but had a friend who also wanted to play. "Bring her along for the ride of her life," Schmirler joked at the time. Gudereit came along. They carried around with them the "Curling Rat from Hell," the rubber rodent that would be their good-luck charm. The following season, their first together, they won their first Saskatchewan women's title. They were on their way.

And it's not over yet. The team has stuck together, and in 1998 made its sixth trip to the Scott in eight years. They are still chasing glory and have set their sights on a second trip to the Olympics and another gold in 2002.

Al Hackner

Al Hackner has made an indelible mark in curling. He won world titles in 1982 and 1985, and is the third-most wins for a skip in Brier history. But, in introspective moments, Hackner admits there might have been more, much more, had he been a little more disciplined.

"I'll be the first to admit I probably wasn't disciplined enough," Hackner says today. "It's no secret I enjoyed myself. I never met a party I didn't like. When I played seriously, we'd always have beer and the stereo going. But that was always the tradeoff. I had a lot of fun playing this game, but I know I could have done more with a little more self-discipline."

Still, he enjoyed a fabulous career and had the time of his life along the way.

"Geez, I've had a hell of a lot of fun playing this game," he says, thinking back to his glory days, which began with his first Brier appearance in 1980. "I've been to a lot of places, made great friends, won some money . . . what's not to be happy about? I have no regrets."

Well, maybe one. Hackner wishes he had a manager, or coach, or somebody, to help guide him following his world-championship years. "I really think we needed somebody to say 'no' once in a while. As defending world champions we were always invited somewhere to curl. It was like being on one big holiday. A free holiday. It was great and we had a lot of fun, but it certainly made it tough to focus on winning again."

It was no coincidence that, following his two world championship years, it took him two years to get back to the Brier.

But Hackner had no trouble focusing when he did make it to a world championship, even when it was in an exotic locale like Garmisch-Partenkirchen, Germany, in 1982.

"Garmisch was fabulous," says Hackner, who was accompanied by his crew of third Rick Lang, second Bob Nichols, and lead Bruce Kennedy. "We were all a bunch of small-town guys from Thunder Bay. So we were all a little wide-eyed. It was the whole Bavarian atmosphere . . . from the resort hotel we stayed in, the mountains, the people. It was like living a fairy tale."

Except on the ice, where it was all business.

Al Hackner judging the sweep at the 1985 Brier in Moncton.

"It's not like the world championships today," Hackner says. "There were only four or five good teams back then, and we knew we could win half our games by just showing up. We had a good attitude going in. We set our sights on just making the playoffs, knowing we would be tough to beat once we got there."

Hackner, who was called "The Iceman" for his coolness under pressure, is particularly proud of not "blowing" his two world-championship appearances. "When you're from Canada, you're expected to win." he says. "Finishing second is nothing."

Lang was the team's conscience. He was on Bill Tetley's Canadian team that lost the world championship in 1975, and kept reminding Hackner and the others how terrible it felt to lose. "He told us he blew it and we weren't going to go back to Canada if we blew it this time," Hackner says. "So we didn't."

Hackner says the notoriety of being world champion has been great, especially in a smaller city like Thunder Bay. "Everybody got to know us. You'd meet people on the street you didn't know who would shake your hand and thank you for winning. I never appreciated what winning meant until several years later."

There were drawbacks, too. "I used to get crank calls from loonies," he says. "It was only recently that I got my number listed in the phone book again."

Hackner won his second world championship in 1985, but his title in Glasgow, Scotland, was nothing compared to what happened weeks earlier, at the Moncton Brier. They still talk about the miraculous double he made for two in the tenth end against Alberta's Pat Ryan that sent the final into a dramatic extra end. It is generally regarded as the most spectacular shot in Brier history.

"I could only see maybe an eighth of the rock," Hackner remembers. "But I said to myself in the hack that I've made that shot before, and if I was ever going to make it again, this was the time."

Ryan came up an inch short in the extra end, and Hackner was on his way to another world championship, this time with Ian Tetley and Pat Perroud as his front end.

Hackner says his Brier win in 1985 evened the books, because he lost the Canadian title in 1981 to Manitoba's Kerry Burtnyk in the last end, when the youthful Winnipegger scored a miraculous three in the final end to win 5-4. "I felt it was fair. I lost a tough one, I won a tough one. These things have a way of evening out," he says.

The Iceman isn't sure he'll ever get back to a Brier again, never mind a world championship. "I don't work at it hard enough," he says of his routine these days. "How you going to win when you don't play or practice enough? But I've had a blast. Two world championships is plenty for anybody."

But how many more could he have won?

Connie Laliberte

During the many years Connie Laliberte has played at the top level in curling, she has had a fairly simple philosophy: You get out of the sport what you put into it. And she's put in a lot.

Laliberte burst onto the scene in 1984, when she skipped her Winnipeg team to a Canadian title. She added the world crown in Perth, Scotland, walloping Switzerland by a score of 10-0 in the final. She has been a dominant figure in the sport ever since, skipping teams in five subsequent Canadian championships and two more world championships (1992 and 1995). In all, she has appeared in seven Canadian championships. Her first exposure to the nationals was as lead for Donna Brownridge of Manitoba in 1980.

Laliberte's game temperament, attitude, and concentration are collectively something special. It is why, almost two decades after her first Tournament of Hearts title, she is still at the top of her game.

"Connie is one of the most determined people I have ever met," says former teammate Cathy Gauthier. "I've never met anyone quite like her. When she puts her mind to something, she does it. She was determined to have a great delivery. She succeeded. She was determined to win a world title. She succeeded. Now she's determined to win another world title. I have no doubt she will."

Laliberte seems at her best when the going gets tough. In 1993 she endured arthroscopic knee surgery and appeared done for the season. Five weeks later, with a more upright delivery, she was on the ice preparing Team Canada for the Scott Tournament of Hearts.

Her brilliant career, of course, has not been without heartache. She has won only once in three tries at the world championship. "It's disappointing," she says, "but people have to understand it's not automatic for Canada anymore. The Europeans are very, very tough. On any given day they can beat you."

Failing to win the Ford Worlds final in Brandon was particularly painful. Laliberte wanted to win in front of friends, family, and a national television audience, but she couldn't get the job done, losing to Swedish nemesis Elisabet Gustafson 6-5 in an extra end. The Canadians had control of the game from the outset, but a 100-1 shot raise to the four-foot gave Gustafson a steal in the ninth end and she subsequently stole the tenth and eleventh.

The next day, Laliberte had to face a bold headline in a Winnipeg paper that read: "Connie Chokes." She shrugged off the home-town blow. "Actually, it bothered my teammates more than me," she recalled. "It just showed me that whoever wrote the headline knows nothing about the game."

Or Laliberte. Women in competitive curling speak of several ways to win—by aggression, by intimidation, by quiet confidence. Laliberte wins with all of them. The bigger the shot, the better she enjoys the game. She won the 1995 Scott final in Calgary with a pressure-packed tap-back to beat Edmonton's Cathy Borst. "If I would have thought about it, I probably would

Connie Laliberte releases with her perfectly balanced, trademark delivery during the finals of the 1992 Scott Tournament of Hearts in Halifax.

have missed it," she says. "I try to use a lot of imagery. I don't think about the result, just the shot. That way, I take the pressure out of it."

Opponents say Laliberte is tough to play because she's absolutely unflappable on the ice. She withdraws behind a poker face, then refuses to allow anything to prick a hole in her concentration. Because opponents can't read her, they never know what she's feeling. Is she in pain? Is she vulnerable? Or is she feeling joy at tearing her opponents to shreds?

You never know with Laliberte. And there's no use asking. She never admits to anything—hence the name "Ice Queen" and the perception of a cold, heartless curling machine. "That's me, I guess," she says, shrugging her shoulders. "If anybody saw me outside the game they'd know I'm pretty much the same way. I don't rant and rave. I don't want people to perceive me as a negative person."

Some day, Laliberte will retire from competitive curling, and the world will lose a great and gracious champion. But right now she remains at the top of her game. She's not ready to yield anything to anybody.

Elisabet Gustafson

Elisabet Gustafson is undoubtedly the finest female shotmaker Sweden has ever produced. After winning an unprecedented fourth world women's title in 1999, she has also proven to be one of the best to ever play the game. She has shared the domination of world women's curling in the 1990s with Sandra Schmirler of Canada and, to a lesser extent, Dordi Nordby of Norway. Between them, they have won all but one of the global titles up for grabs in the decade.

So what is left for Gustafson to accomplish in the sport? Five titles? Six? Seven? She still has the skill and the team to win again and again at the world level, but where's the motivation? Much of it comes from her status as a national hero in Sweden. Gustafson believes she has an obligation to help the sport grow in her country. "It's very important for Swedish curling to capitalize on all the attention our team has been getting," Gustafson said shortly after winning her record fourth title. "I'm sure we'll see lots more curlers in the future."

Gustafson has been getting her share of attention with world titles in 1992, 1995, 1998, and 1999. She has been to six world championships in this decade and brought home the bronze medal at the 1998 Nagano Olympics. It was at the Olympics that she fully understood the impact she was having on a nation of eight million. Her bronze-medal game was televised live at 6:00 A.M. in Stockholm, and 765,000 viewers tuned in.

"It's not a very big sport in Sweden, only 5,000 licensed curlers," says Katarina Sjoberg, a two-time European champion and two-time world championship finalist who is now a Swedish TV reporter. "But Elisabet really caused a boom in interest."

Gustafson is a perfect role model for the sport in Sweden. She works as a surgeon in Orebro, but still finds the time necessary to devote to her sport.

Elisabet Gustafson of Sweden is the only curler in the world to skip a team to four world women's championship titles.

She has a tremendous will to win, but would never imagine breaking up her team to do it. Katarina Nyberg, Louise Marmont, and Elisabeth Persson have been with Gustafson throughout the 1990s. They are all good friends and work hard at their game, traveling great distances to play together. "There is a lot of traveling," Gustafson admits. "but it hasn't been a disadvantage. Every time you enter a tournament, you think you can win."

Gustafson was the first to take up the game in 1980. Television provided her introduction to the sport. "I became interested watching the Silver Broom in Karlstad on television in 1977," she says. It helped that Swede Ragnar Kamp won the world championship that year.

Gustafson formed her team in the early 1980s, persuading her best friend Persson to take up the game, then recruiting Nyberg. With Eva-Lena Jonsson, they became the first junior women's team in Umea. But it wasn't until Marmont joined the team in 1990 that big things began to happen. They lost the Swedish final that year, but two years later began a string of championships that may never be equalled.

Ed Werenich, Brier world champion, 1983 and 1990.

Ed Werenich

Many people have said that Ed Werenich does not look like your typical athlete. Nevertheless, Werenich has parlayed a fierce competitiveness and uncanny skill into one of the most successful and colorful careers in the history of Canadian curling.

The feisty Scarborough, Ontario, firefighter, a two-time world curling champion, was a veteran of national firefighter curling championships when he first showed up at the Brier as second for Toronto's Paul Savage in 1973. It was Werenich's first of ten Brier appearances, matching him with three other Canadian curlers who have hit double figures in terms of Brier participation. And there's no reason to think he's done yet. That's how deep the fires burn inside the man they call "The Wrench."

Werenich was born to skip, although his first three trips to the Brier with Savage in 1973, 1974, and 1977 were as either second or third. But it wasn't until he broke away from Savage to skip his own team that Werenich's ability became clear. He has, over the years, developed the skill of an old chess master. Opponents talk about the way he thinks his way through the game, always working the angles and possibilities. "He's incredibly crafty," says Alberta's Kevin Martin, who has locked horns with Werenich many times. "He loves to get rocks in play and he's the best there is at that game. I think he enjoys moving stones around. Then, all of a sudden, bang, he's got you."

Werenich skipped the Ontario Tankard champs for the first time in 1981 and finished 7-5 and out of the money. Two years later, he was back with Savage at third, John Kawaja at second and Neil Harrison at lead to win his first Canadian title. It was the start of the Werenich era in Canadian curling, a period filled with heaps of controversy, high-octane quotes and plenty of great curling.

"The Wrench." It is one of sport's all-time great nicknames. It has a solid, blue-collar feel to it, and that's Werenich, right down to the toothpick stuck between his teeth. He's always been a battler and scrapper, ever since his days in tiny Benito, Manitoba, where he learned the game in grade school. He likes to play the role of the gritty underdog and has never been afraid to speak his mind. If it rubs some people the wrong way, Werenich doesn't seem to care. He's had several dust-ups with opponents at the Brier and world championships, battled with his own teammates and been a constant thorn in the side of Canadian curling officials. There is nobody in curling Werenich won't take on if he thinks he's been wronged.

One of his most celebrated rows came after his 1983 Brier win. Werenich represented Canada at the world curling championships in Regina where he ran into the Swedes skipped by Stefan Hasselborg. Werenich became testy with the Swedes over etiquette and corn broom chaffe, and let them have it with both barrels. "Those guys know nothing about sportsmanship and etiquette," he told the press. "I can't believe the stunts they pull . . . It'd be easy for us to say nothing, but I chastised these guys and I think they deserve it." The controversy only ratcheted up Werenich's resolve to win. He knocked off West Germany's Keith Wendorf in the final to win his first world title.

Werenich became a media darling after Regina, and it worked both ways. The press loved his candor; The Wrench loved the way he could stir things up with a few short syllables. Of sports psychology and the benefit of getting in shape, he once said: "We're not into it. We see food, we eat it. We see something to drink, we drink it. Then we go to bed."

Werenich's second Brier and world successes came in 1990, after failed trips in 1984 and 1988. Werenich earned his second trip to the worlds with Kawaja at third, and front-enders Ian Tetley and Pat Perroud from Al Hackner's 1985 world champion Thunder Bay team. Ironically, the worlds were held in Vasteras, Sweden. Werenich, as usual, was candid about a trip to Hasselborg's native country.

The wily veteran has been back for two more shots in the 1990s at his third Brier title, but failed to reach the final in either sortie.

Cathy Borst

At the moment of her triumph, Cathy Borst flashed-back through her life. It was a long time between wins. Twenty years had passed since she won back-to-back titles at the Canadian junior championship. Those years, 1977 and 1978, seemed so long ago, a time when there was no chance to go onto a world-championship shot.

There had been many sacrifices along the way, terrible tolls in her personal life. But, in the end, if only for that moment when she made her last shot against Anne Merklinger to win the 1998 Scott Tournament of Hearts, there was a "damn it, this was all worth it" feeling.

"It took a lot of sacrifices for a lot of different things," said Borst. "Your kids, your husband, your friends. There is a price to pay. The moment we'd made that shot, in one way I felt it was all worth it, because it was one of the happiest moments of my life."

Her love affair with the game began back in 1974. Her older brothers, Robb and Chris King, had won the Canadian junior title and represented Canada at the Worlds in 1974 and 1975. Her mom, June, was a curling coach. The family lived in a upper-middle-class neighborhood in West Edmonton.

"I was their biggest fan," said Borst. "I was into the games, into the strategy and everything, even at that age."

Young Cathy was named athlete of the year in her Grade 9 junior high school. If there was a sport, she wanted to be part of it. She was a bronze-medallion swimmer, gymnast, track competitor, fastball player, and co-captain of the high-school volleyball team.

"Miss Jockette, they called me," said Borst, who teamed up with another jockette, Maureen Olson, for her two titles. "At that age, if you're coordinated in a lot of sports, curling will come easy. For me, it was the strategy I really enjoyed. We had a great team right off the start. We were just a powerhouse. We were on fire. Everybody could see that when they came to play us."

The 1980s were a dark time. After a year off, the junior team reunited and finished Alberta runner-up in 1980. But, eventually, Olson moved away and real life beckoned. The magic went into remission.

"I got married, had three children," said Borst. "I remember playing zones one year, seven months' pregnant." Being a mom took priority. Looking after her sons, Karston, Travis, and Kyle, became her main focus.

But, it was shortly after the birth of Kyle that the competitive call began beckoning. By 1993, the elements of her first Scotts team were starting to come together.

She threw third rocks for Maureen Brown on a team that had Kate Horne at lead and that lost the C qualifier out of Edmonton. The next year, Deanne Shields was added at second, and the team made it all the way to the provincial final. The following year, that foursome won the province.

Borst became Canada's darling at the Scotts after enduring a five game in twenty-seven-hour tiebreakers. Then, she knocked off Sandra Schmirler and Team Canada to advance to the final against Manitoba's Ice Queen, Connie Laliberté. They lost by a rock that stuck in the 12-foot.

"We had a lot of people just come on our side just for that reason, feeling sorry for us and wanting that underdog team, which had worked so hard, to win," said Borst.

The next year, Shields left the team, and Brenda Bohmer took over at second. But this time, Cheryl Kullman came out on top to represent the province.

In 1997, the team made a key move when Heather Godberson joined fresh off a win at the world juniors. The Olympic Trials was the focus, and Brown felt she could not commit the necessary time. The 1997 Scotts in Vancouver became a bust after Borst lost a tiebreaker to Laura Phillips of Newfoundland.

After going down to their last life at the city level, the team ran a 13-game streak to win the province in 1998, and were hot going into the Scotts.

"We were ready, we had unfinished business," said Borst. "I know I didn't play well myself in Vancouver. I was all-star at provincials, but couldn't come through at the Scotts. In 1998, I looked at the field and thought, 'This could be our year.' There was Sandra Schmirler and Anne Merklinger. Sure enough, it came down to us three teams."

After a hand-of-fate 1-2 playoff-game win against Merklinger, the final was phenomenal, and the atmosphere electric.

"Don't ask me how we ever got into that [dancing the macarena during a break]," said Borst. "We were having such a good time in that game."

Former junior champs had gone on to win ladies' titles. But twenty years is a long time . . .

"It was like a gnawing thing in my brain," Borst said. "I can't believe I persisted that long to realize my dream."

The team went on to the worlds at Kamloops, British Columbia—a circus the likes of which Borst had never seen before. "We were not really aware of the differences—of what a world championship [versus] a Canadian championship would be like," Borst said. "It is a totally different atmosphere. You're playing different rules. Half the teams don't speak English. It was a real eye-opener."

The Canadians walked away with a bronze after taking eventual champ Elisabet Gustafsson to an extra end in the semi and pummeling former world champ Dordi Nordby in the bronze-medal game.

The team still remains humble and, in some ways, fragile despite its success. They still have not developed the championship swagger and the aura of power that distinguished the Schmirler team.

In some ways, they're an unlikely combination. But, that's the way they like it.

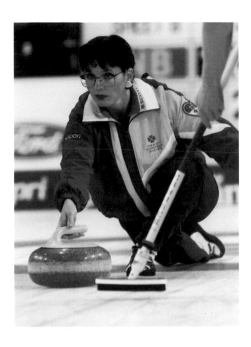

Cathy Borst won the Canadian Junior Women's title for Alberta in 1977 and 1978.

Pat Ryan

What are a curler's most important attributes? Patience and mental toughness come to mind. Pat Ryan had them in spades, which is one of the main reasons he has won just about every important prize men's curling has to offer.

But there was one prize he was never even close to winning: the hearts of curling fans in Alberta.

Ryan, who won five Alberta championships, two Briers, and a world championship in a brilliant thirteen-year stay in the Alberta capital, must surely rank as one of the greatest curlers to wear Alberta's Wild Rose emblem on his back. But in the arena of public affection, he was no Hec Gervais. Or, for that matter, Paul Gowsell or Matt Baldwin.

Despite all his championships and media attention, Albertans had a tough time holding Ryan to their collective bosoms. It wasn't until the final couple of years of his stay in Edmonton, before he bolted to the gentler climate of Kelowna, that Albertans started to warm up to Ryan and his marvelous talent.

"It takes a while to get adopted," says Ryan, who is now living the good life in British Columbia. "I think it wasn't until we lost the 1985 Brier that people started to think of my team as an Alberta team. Let's see . . . that's about nine years."

The question is: Why did it take so long?

"I think partly that's my fault," admits Ryan, looking in the rear-view mirror at the Edmonton years. "I never was the most colorful guy in the sport. I was just a regular guy who liked to curl and who was pretty good at it. I was never really all that comfortable in the spotlight."

Okay, so he wasn't as quotable as Gowsell, or as down-home friendly as Gervais, or as colorful as Baldwin. Lots of curlers are lunch-bucket guys. So there has to be some other underlying reason to explain why a curler of Ryan's abilities failed to capture the imagination of Albertans, or why—horror of horrors—fans were capable of booing him at a hometown Brier in Edmonton.

It could be Albertans had a hard time accepting Ryan because he was not one of their own. He was an interloper, born and raised in Winnipeg, where he cut his curling teeth and earned his first provincial championship as a high-schooler in 1973.

Ryan ended up in Edmonton, like a lot of Canadians, following a career path. He accepted an accounting job with Imperial Oil in 1976, and set into motion one of Canada's great curling careers.

"I went to Edmonton for a job," said Ryan, "but curling was never far out of my mind. I never set out to be a world champ, or anything. But I loved the game, had some success, and knew I wanted to play."

Edmonton's curling establishment quickly took notice of the new kid in town. It wasn't hard. That tuck slide that Ryan brought with him was a dead giveaway that his roots were in Manitoba.

But Ryan showed them plenty more than a corkscrew delivery. It was clear the young man could curl.

Ryan played with an old friend, Derek Devlin, another ex-Manitoban, in his first season in Edmonton, and the team they stitched together at the Crestwood Club was immediately competitive. Soon, Ryan was throwing second stones for Paul Devlin's team, which included third John Hunter and Derek Devlin at lead.

It didn't help their assimilation into mainstream Alberta curling that all four members were ex-Manitobans.

Devlin's team won the Alberta men's title in 1979, and Ryan says he knew then that acceptance would be hard to come by.

"When we finally won the province," says Ryan, "the fella making the trophy presentation at the time said in his speech that it was too bad that there would be two Manitoba teams in the Brier that year.

"I'd like to point out," Ryan added, "that we had been living in Edmonton for three years at the time."

Pat Ryan won two Briers (1988, 1989) as a skip playing out of Edmonton, and one as third for Rick Folk (1994) with the Kelowna Curling Club at home base. He is considered by many to be the best all-round curler and shotmaker of the 1980s and 1990s.

Devlin finished with a so-so 6-5 record that year in Ottawa, the last of the Macdonald Briers. Ryan had a taste of the big time and he liked it. He continued to play for Devlin for a couple more years, but the urge to skip finally took over, and he piloted his own squad in 1982, curling out of the Ottewell Club.

Three years later he was back in the Brier, where he learned a lesson that would stay with him for the remainder of his career.

Ryan, who by now had a lineup of Gord Trenchie, Don Walchuk, and Don McKenzie in front of him, tore through the 1985 Brier field in Moncton. The Albertans piled up an amazing 11-0 round-robin record, outscored the opposition 2-1, never yielded more than two points on an end, and allowed only one steal all week. They hit, they peeled, they did everything but clean the ice between draws.

They even earned a new nickname: Ryan's Express.

But they couldn't win the big one, losing the final to Thunder Bay's Al Hackner.

"We blew the Brier final because we couldn't defend against the lead," said Ryan. "So we learned from that mistake and vowed to become the best peeling team ever. We really went to work on that part of the game."

And with it came yet another knock against Ryan. His team executed defense so efficiently that some of their games became an unappealing series of peels and takeouts. It was a style that would eventually take them to the top of the curling mountain.

First, though, was an embarrassing Brier appearance at the Edmonton Agridome in 1987, where Ryan finished 6-5 and was lustily booed in one particular game.

"Do I remember it? You bet," Ryan said, his voice rising. "It's not something you'd forget."

Ryan says the whole Edmonton Brier experience was a bummer. "We never quite got the feel of things," he said. "I think we were defocused because we were playing in Edmonton. We had higher expectations and wanted to win for the home crowd. It was very disappointing."

Ryan insists the booing incident was started by some Edmonton curlers he knew in the crowd who were into their cups and wanted to have some fun at his expense.

"At the time we didn't react very well to it and that probably helped them boo some more," said Ryan. "It started off with a few of them but, soon it was the whole crowd."

That would be the last time Ryan would be embarrassed at a Brier. His teams won back-to-back Briers in 1988 and 1989, adding the world title in magnificent style the second year.

His Brier win in 1989 marked the dawn of a new era for the sport. By now Ryan, Randy Ferbey, Walchuk, and McKenzie had the peel game down to an exact science. They beat Rick Folk's B.C. squad 3-2 in a mind-numbing final in Saskatoon that had precious little action.

No boos rained down this time. Instead, Ryan endured a chorus of "borrrrrring" from the crowd.

By then curling officials had seen enough. That game may have had a lot to do with the introduction of the Free Guard Zone (FGZ) rule.

Ryan figures his team got a bad rap for its defensive style of play.

"People think we were boring," said Ryan, "but most teams we played would say we were among the most aggressive teams they ever played. They knew that if they put a guard up, we were going around it.

"We may have had the widest range in game styles. We could play with a lot of aggressiveness, a lot of come-arounds and freezes. Almost the kind of game we see today, with the Free Guard Zone rule. But as soon as we got up a point and had hammer, we could peel it clean and end the game. That didn't just happen. We worked hard, practiced and honed our skills on that part of the game."

Ryan says the championships were great, but some of his best memories of his stay in Edmonton were knocking heads with the top teams in Alberta at the time.

"There would be some absolutely great games against guys like Tommy Reed, Ed Lukowich, and Paul Gowsell," Ryan said. "They helped shape the way I played the game, and the way I focused. It was a great learning experience. Edmonton was a great place to play."

Ryan, who is now comfortably entrenched in Kelowna and still playing great in his mid-forties, says leaving Edmonton in 1989 was difficult.

"It was really hard. I always felt I was going to live in Edmonton the rest of my life," he says. "There were so many people I became close with, in curling and in work. That was the hardest part of leaving."

Ryan joined up with another former Brier champion, Rick Folk, when he moved to Kelowna, and the combination of Folk skipping, with Ryan at third, represented the province at the Brier in 1994 and 1995. In 1994 the foursome, with Bert Gretzinger at second and Gerry Richards at lead, won the Brier and the world championship. For both Folk and Ryan, it was the second world win.

Russ Howard

The burden of excellence in sports has always been about winning. The best athletes are always expected to win the biggest and best championships. If they do not, their abilities are questioned.

Russ Howard's abilities were certainly questioned following the 1986 Brier where he had a chance to win the biggest and best championship of them all the Brier. He was even questioning himself after his Ontario squad lost a heartbreaking final 4-3 to Alberta's Ed Lukowich.

"You can't believe what goes through your head when you lose the Brier final for the first time," Howard would say. "How many times are you going to get a shot?"

Russ Howard with his patented vocal cords in full volume.

Plenty, as it turns out. The burden no longer exists. The questions about Howard's ability and his place in history were answered years ago. Howard went on to win the Brier the very next year after his close call, and there has been no looking back ever since.

Howard is now up there on a plateau with the greatest skips who ever played the game. He is a two-time Canadian and world champion and has the all-time winning record for a skip in Brier history with sixty-eight wins. How's that for meeting the burden of excellence?

"But you could never have convinced me it would have turned out that way after losing to Lukowich," Howard says, looking back. "It was like it was my one and only chance."

Curling is full of stories of players who have their brush with greatness and are never heard from again. Howard wasn't sure he would be one of them after his close call in 1986. But he had several things going for him at the time. He was a technically perfect curler, he had a brilliant mind for the game, and he had a fierce appetite for success. They made for a formidable combination of abilities.

Howard was never the most popular champion, at least in the beginning. Perhaps it was his serious mien and the scream in his voice that turned some people against the skip from Penetanguishene, Ont. He showed up at his first Brier in 1980 with a wet-behind-the-ears Ontario team that struggled to a 5-6 record, but all anybody could remember about them was the screaming of "haaaaaard!" that came from Howard's mouth. It would become his anthem and his enemy over the years.

"I have a speech therapist who says I could lose my voice permanently if I keep curling," says Howard. "I have to be careful."

By the time Howard made it to his second Brier in 1986, six years had passed. The screaming was still there, but this time Howard had his younger brother Glenn, his curling alter ego, at his side. It was a key change in the lineup. The Howard brothers would form one of curling's great brother acts over the years.

Howard feels he should have won that year. "I had a chance for two in the ninth. I hit and rolled out by about an inch. Ed (Lukowich) beat us on the last shot. The dream was over."

Actually, it was just about to begin. He was back the following year in exactly the same position. "We climbed the mountain again, after people had told us all summer that I must have choked, that I was nervous. So here I am, exactly one year later, and I've got a wide-open hit to beat Bernie Sparkes for the title. I sat in the hack thinking . . . We got all the way to the top of the mountain twice and I felt we better do it this time or we might not see the mountain again."

This time there were no mistakes. Howard went on to win the Brier and capped a tremendous season with a victory in the world championship in Vancouver. He added a second Canadian and world title in 1993. His other Brier years with Ontario were in 1989, 1991, 1992, and 1994.

Some people thought it was over for Howard, especially after he moved from Ontario to take a golf pro job in Moncton, New Brunswick, in 1998. But, as usual, he fooled them all. He cobbled together a team in Moncton and made it to his ninth Brier in 1999. He didn't win, but he made it interesting.

Howard has also been one of the game's great innovators. It was his idea to come up with the Moncton Rule, called thus because it was first used in competition in the Moncton 100 bonspiel in 1990. He was also responsible for a rule change in 1989 when he was heading the Ontario team at his fourth Brier. As usual, he lost his voice by screaming. To combat the problem, he picked up headsets at Radio Shack. No one even noticed until his instructions jammed the officials' walkie-talkies. Hauled into a meeting, he was told the headsets were a no-no and they had to go. Howard countered that there was no such rule in the book. It was added midway through the Brier and now states no communication devices can be used.

Rules and Etiquette

I'm a firm believer in fair play and keeping the playing surface as level as possible for all curlers. That's why I urged the Canadian Curling Association (CCA) rules committee in the late 1970s to deal with players who show little regard for a number of curling's common rules and courtesies.

Some traditionalists argue that curling is a gentleman's game and the players should be left alone to police themselves. But how do you deal with a situation where the majority choose to follow the curling code of ethics while others do not?

I finally got my message through in 1979 and, while the rules committee would not agree to enforce the rules at the 1980 Brier, it did allow a number of observers who would simply record all rule violations, but without penalty. The result was mind-boggling, even for curling traditionalists. More than 3,000 violations were recorded at the week-long event. Many were minor violations involving positioning and movement, but more than 120 were serious violations of the hog-line rule. The CCA rules committee took notice and, to the dismay of many, officiating and rules enforcement made its first appearance at the 1981 Brier.

Between 1981 and 1985, enforcement was carried out by warning the violators and threatening suspension. However, violators were not getting the message, so the CCA officiating team entered the 1986 Brier with the power to enforce. By the end of the championship, nearly fifty stones had been removed from play by the officials for hog-line violations.

Officiating and enforcement continues today in all of the CCA championships. It is interesting to note that events such as the World Curling Tour and other major bonspiels still operate without officials. That's a mistake. A sport that does not enforce its own rules will have trouble earning credibility as a legitimate sport.

Curling, like golf, has been guided over time by many courtesies and traditions. A sense of personal integrity has been part of competition at all levels. It is one of the few sports in the world that starts and ends with a customary handshake. To ensure that all curlers are aware of their personal responsibilities when playing the game, the CCA has adopted a code of ethics as an official supplement to its rules of the game.

CURLERS' CODE OF ETHICS

- I will play the game with a spirit of good sportsmanship;

- I will conduct myself in an honorable manner both on and off the ice;

- I will never knowingly break a rule, but if I do, I will divulge the breach;

- I will take no action that could be interpreted as an attempt to intimidate or demean my opponents, teammates, or officials;

- I will interpret the rules in an impartial manner, always keeping in mind that the purpose of the rules is to ensure that the game is played in an orderly and fair manner;

- I will humbly accept any penalty that the governing body at any level of curling deems appropriate, if I am found in violation of the code of ethics or rules of the game.

There have always been differences in the way the CCA and World Curling Federation (WCF) operate. In recent years those differences have increased. Most curling is basically played without the use of officials or any sort of organized game control. The CCA has developed a set of rules that are defined as "Rules of General Play" and come without any suggestion that a penalty might exist for violation. It is expected that, in keeping with the traditions of the game, curlers will police themselves. To deal with the demands of competitive play, the CCA has also put together a set of rules for officiated competition known as "Rules of Curling for Officiated Play." The World Curling Federation does not use a two-rule-book system but controls play at all levels with one set of general rules.

The differences between the CCA and WCF rules begin with the actual size of the sheet of ice. In Canada, a sheet of curling ice is 146 feet (45 m) long by 14 feet 2 inches (4.3 m) wide (Fig. 4.1). The sheet of ice at the world level is wider, at 15 feet 4 inches (4.7 m). Why the difference in width? It comes down to the construction of buildings in Canada, where five sheets of ice can be crammed into the space of four if the dividers are eliminated and the width reduced by an additional 8 inches (20 cm) per sheet. The Europeans have always argued that the sheet divider in Canada serves as a guard for a rock that is close to the outer circle on one side and the divider on the other.

Another marking on the ice that differs between the WCF and the CCA is the use of the back-line (Fig. 4.2). In Canada, the back-line is one-half inch (12.7 cm) in width and drawn so that its inner edge (closest to the button) touches the outer edge of the 12-foot circle, where the two intersect near the back line (Fig. 4.3). The WCF rule has the outer edge of the 12-foot circle touching the outer edge of the back line where the two intersect, at the point where the back line meets the center line.

Top: Figure 4.1

Middle: Figure 4.2

Bottom: Figure 4.3

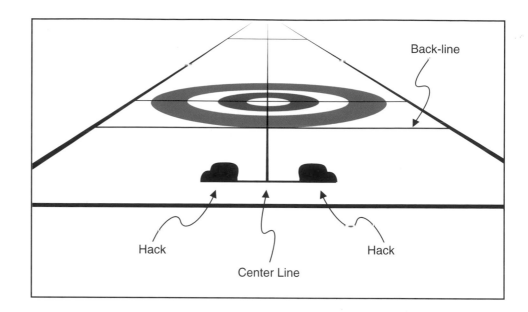

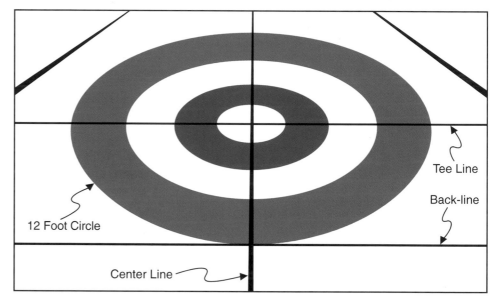

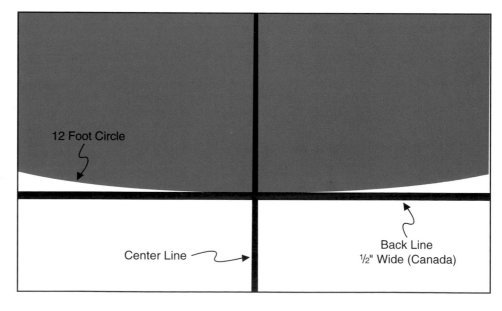

THE RINK

Some people claim that curling is a one-rule sport. They speak, of course, of the hog line, the line that is scribed across the sheet 33 feet (10 m) from each hack. The hog line was initially used in curling to determine whether or not a rock was in or out of play. It had absolutely no connection to the delivery. The fact is that the hog line never came into play during the delivery because, when the game originated, players threw from a stationary mat known as a crampit.

But the game changed. In the late 1930s and 1940s, a school teacher from Winnipeg named Ken Watson discovered that sliding from the hack improved shot-making accuracy. Watson and his teammates never ventured beyond the tee line, but others did. A new crowd was developing a sliding style that propelled them practically from one end of the sheet to the other. The Dominion Curling Association (now the CCA) took notice in 1954, when youthful Stan Austman of Kenaston, Saskatchewan, glided from hack to far tee line at the Canadian schoolboy championship. Austman placed the rock smack on the button on his slide by.

It was obvious the DCA would have to confront the issue. At its annual meeting in 1955, Rule 16 was written to officially recognize the hog line as a dual-purpose ice marking. Here is how the initial rule was written: "Each player must play from the hack and in the delivery of the stone no player shall go beyond the hogline nearest the hack from which the player is playing." No mention was made about the release of the stone or any part of the body passing the hog line.

The rule received its first official revision in 1957. It read: "Each player must play from the hack and in the delivery of the stone no part of the foot on which the player is sliding shall touch the nearest hogline."

Problems remained with the word "touch" because some players were becoming proficient at lifting their sliding feet over the line and continuing to slide with the rock. In 1958, the DCA passed yet another rule revision: "Each player must play from the hack and in the delivery of the stone, the foot on which the player is sliding must not cross the hogline."

Over a span of the next few years, various discussions on the rule were heard. They led to still another rewrite in 1962: "Each player must play from the hack and in the delivery of the stone, no part of the curler's body shall go beyond the nearest hogline during the uninterrupted motion in the delivery of the stone. Nor shall the curler be permitted to leap over, slide over on the other foot or even put a hand over to check the slide."

Between 1963 and 1972, the wording of the rule changed only slightly, primarily to add: "In the event of an infraction, the stone shall be removed from the ice by the playing side." For the first time in history, the administrative body was suggesting a penalty for violation of the hog-line rule. The ICF horned into the argument in 1973 and made it known that, starting with the 1974 world men's championship, the player would be required to release the rock by the hog line and could continue to slide for as long as desired.

Since 1974, the wording of the rule has been altered only slightly. During the late 1970s, the hog line was not enforced, but the rules committee of the CCA decided to determine the extent of violations and introduced umpires at the 1980 Brier in Calgary. More than 120 blatant violations of the hog-line rule were observed. The CCA decided to turn the screws tighter and, by the 1986 Brier, full enforcement was in place.

In recent years a number of players complained that the hog-line rule did not give the player the benefit of the doubt. So, with that in mind, the CCA made one more change in 1998. The hog-line rule now reads: "In the delivery of the stone, the player's hand shall be released from all parts of the stone before the stone has completely crossed the nearer hogline." In essence, the hog-line rule has been extended about 16 inches (40 cm) in an attempt to make it easier for the curler to abide.

The WCF, on the other hand, decided to continue with the old hog-line rule, just one more difference between CCA and WCF rules.

Today, enforcement is a standard element of the game's officiating procedure for all Canadian and world events. Opponents of enforcement should keep this in mind. The game of curling was designed on a pond many years ago, and the objective was to deliver a stone from a foothold to a mark 146 feet (45 m) away. The point is, the closer the curler is allowed to move toward the target, the less skill is involved and the less credibility the game has. In order to maintain the integrity of the sport, the hog-line rule must be enforced.

In the "Rules of Curling for General Play," the penalty for violation is that "the delivered stone and all affected stones must come to rest before any action may take place. If a team declares its own violation, the non-offending team shall remove the stone just delivered from play and replace all affected stones as close as possible to their original positions."

Under the "Rules of Curling for Officiated Play," the penalty for violation is that "the delivered stone and all affected stones shall come to rest before any action is taken. The official shall remove the stone just delivered from play and replace all affected stones as close as possible to their original position."

TEAMS

A curling team comprises four players, with each player delivering two stones alternately with the opponent during the course of an end (a total of sixteen stones are thrown in a complete end—eight per team). The delivery rotation declared at the beginning of a game must be followed throughout the game unless the rules of the competition allow for a substitute, in which case the rotation may be changed. A team may play with three players, with the first two players each delivering three stones in each end.

Under no circumstance can a team play with fewer than three players delivering stones.

The skip has exclusive direction of the game for his team but may throw stones at any position in the delivery rotation. However, the player designated as skip shall remain in that capacity throughout the game. When it is the skip's turn to deliver, he shall elect a teammate to act as skip. The vice-skip may also play any position in the delivery rotation and must stay in that capacity throughout the course of the game.

POSITION OF PLAYERS

Only the skip and vice-skip may be positioned inside the hog line of the playing end and should remain behind the back line when the opposing team is in the process of delivery. Both players should remain still with their brooms in a position that will not interfere with or distract the attention of the player who is in the process of delivery.

The player next up to deliver a stone should take a position by the backboard at the delivering end and to the side of the sheet. The player must remain silent and motionless when the opposing team player is in the process of delivery.

When the opposing team is in the process of delivery, the two players who aren't skipping or about to throw next should position themselves between the hog lines and to the extreme sides of the sheet, and remain in single file.

The skip or vice-skip of the delivering team is positioned inside the hog line and on the ice surface of the playing end when his or her team is in the process of delivery and has choice of position for the purpose of directing play.

DELIVERY

Right-handed deliveries are initiated from the hack located to the left of the center line, and left-handed deliveries are initiated from the hack located to the right of the center line. Both right- and left-handed deliveries may be initiated from a hack located on the center line.

If a player mistakenly delivers a stone belonging to the opposing team, a stone belonging to his or her team shall be put in its place.

If a player wants to redeliver a stone, as a result of his or her own team's action, he or she may do so providing the stone has not been released from the player's hand and has not reached the nearer tee line (a stone may be replayed if the player's body or equipment reaches the tee line, providing the stone does not).

Delay of a game in progress by a player for any reason, excluding accident or illness, shall not exceed three minutes.

TOUCHED DELIVERED STONE OR STONES SET IN MOTION

A delivered stone or stones, set in motion, shall not be touched by any player, equipment, or personal belongings of the team delivering it. Penalty for this infraction is that the delivered stone or stones set in motion and all affected stones shall come to rest before any action takes place. If a team declares its own violation, then the non-offending team may: (a) allow play to stand; (b) remove the touched stone from play and replace all affected stones as close as possible to their original position; or (c) place the touched stone and all stones it would have affected where they would have come to rest had the violation not occurred. Solution (c) can be applied only if the violation occurred inside the hog line at the end of play.

A delivered stone shall not be touched by any player of the opposing team or their equipment, nor shall the opposing team cause it to be touched. Penalty for this infraction is that the delivered stone or stones set in motion and all affected stones shall come to rest before any action takes place. If a team declares its own violation, then the non-offending team may: (a) allow play to stand; (b) place the touched stone and all stones it would have affected where they would have come to rest had the violation not occurred; or (c) redeliver the stone. Solution (b) can be applied only if the violation occurred inside the hog line at the end of play.

If a delivered stone or stone in the process of delivery is touched or caused to be touched by an external force, that is, stone, broom, or brush from another sheet, spectator, and so on, the player shall redeliver the stone. If the touched stone has displaced other stones, they shall be replaced as close as possible to their original positions to the satisfaction of both teams.

DISPLACED STATIONARY STONES

A stationary stone shall not be displaced by a player or the player's equipment, nor shall a player cause a stone to be displaced by an opposing player or that player's equipment. If a team declares its own violation, the non-offending team shall replace the displaced stone or stones as close as possible to its original position.

If a sweeper is attempting to sweep a rock around a guard and in the process the guard is touched, to a degree that the shooter would not get by, the opposing team may, once all affected stones have come to rest: (a) allow the play to stand as it is; (b) remove the stone just delivered from play as well as any stones set in motion and replace all affected stones as close as possible to their original positions; or (c) place the stone just delivered or stones set in motion and all stones it would have affected where they would have come to rest had the violation not occurred.

A stationary stone cannot be moved by a stone that deflects from a divider or a stone from another sheet. It is the responsibility of the delivering team to stop rocks that deflect from the divider. If a deflecting stone moves a stationary stone in play, once all of the stones have come to rest, the stones are placed back as close as possible to where they originally lay, to the satisfaction of the opposing team.

If the stones in play are displaced by a force other than the two teams playing on a sheet of ice, then both teams should determine the position to which rocks are to be returned. If the teams cannot agree on the positioning of the stones prior to being displaced, then the end must be replayed.

SWEEPING/BRUSHING

Between the tee lines, all members of the delivering team may sweep/brush their team's stones. The Canadian rules state that either the skip or the vice-skip of the non-delivering team may sweep/brush their team's stone(s) after set in motion by a stone of the delivering team. Also, behind the tee line, only one player from each team may sweep/brush at one time. The player could be the skip or vice-skip of either team, or the lead or second of the delivering team (basically, the lead or second who is in motion or has momentum when sweeping a rock that belongs to their team may continue that motion to sweep behind the tee, but only one can continue to sweep beyond the tee).

The WCF sweeping rule is quite different as it pertains to sweeping a rock behind the tee. One sweeper is allowed behind the tee at all times, but only the skip or acting skip in charge of the house at the time (this means that, once the skip goes to deliver, he or she can return to the house for consultation, but the vice-skip retains the sweeping privileges behind the tee for the balance of the end). Behind the tee line, each team has first privilege of sweeping/brushing its own stone. If the choice is not to sweep/brush, that team shall not obstruct or prevent the opponent from sweeping/brushing. An opponent's stone shall not be swept/brushed until it reaches the tee line and shall be swept/brushed only behind the tee line.

The sweeping/brushing motion shall be from side to side and should not leave any debris in front of a delivered stone or a stone set in motion. The final sweeping/brushing motion shall finish to either side of the stone in motion. All sweeping/brushing shall take place within 6 feet (1.8 m) in front of the delivered stone or stone set in motion.

METHOD OF PLAY: FREE GUARD ZONE

The area between the hog line and tee line, excluding the house, is known as the Free Guard Zone (FGZ). A stone which comes to rest touching or in front of the hog line after making contact with a stone in the FGZ is considered to be in the FGZ. A stone that comes to rest outside of the rings but touching the tee line is not in the FGZ.

The FGZ is another area where Canadian and WCF rules differ. Canadians play the Three-Rock FGZ, while the WCF uses a Four-Rock FGZ.

Under Canadian rules, after delivery of the first two rocks of an end it is the responsibility of the skip of the team who is about to deliver to ensure agreement with the opposing skip as to whether or not the stone just delivered has come to rest in the FGZ (in the case of the WCF rules, it is the first three rocks delivered in an end). If the skips cannot agree, they can use the 6-foot (1.8-m) measuring stick. The Canadian rules state that any stationary stone located within the FGZ cannot be removed from play until after the third stone of the end has been delivered. The WCF rules states that the FGZ rule stands for the first four rocks delivered in an end. A delivered third stone of an end may hit a stone in the FGZ onto a stone not in the FGZ providing the original FGZ stone remains in play. If at anytime prior to the fourth rock of the end being delivered an FGZ rock is removed from play, the opponent has the option of allowing play to stand or removing the stone just delivered from play and replacing the displaced stone(s) as close as possible to the original position.

The WCF rule applies to the first four stones of an end rather than the first three. You are also allowed to remove your own stone from the FGZ at all times.

STONES IN PLAY AND SCORING

A stone that does not come to rest inside the inner edge (circle side) of the farther hog line shall be removed from play immediately, except where it has struck another stone lying in play. A stone coming to rest beyond the outer edge of the back line will be removed from play. A stone that touches a side line, hits a divider, or comes to rest biting a side line shall be removed from play immediately. A game shall be decided by the majority of points scored. Each stone, any part of which is within 6 feet (1.8 m) of the tee, is eligible to be counted.

A team scores one point for each stone that it has closer to the tee than any opposition stone. An end is decided when the skips or vice-skips in charge of the house agree on the score for the end just completed. If a possible scoring stone is displaced prior to the skips or vice-skips deciding the score, the team causing the displacement will forfeit the points involved.

All curlers should know the rules in detail. Once you have learned the basics, contact your national curling association and purchase a rule book.

The Fundamentals

EQUIPMENT

Footwear

Curling, like most sports, requires the proper equipment for comfort, safety, and success. Today, there are various levels of quality, and cost. It is smart to pay a little extra to ensure you get a pair of shoes that are comfortable, a brush that doesn't shed, and a pair of gloves that allow you to feel the rock through them.

The sliding shoe is probably the most important piece of equipment that you will invest in. Ideally, the shoe will be equipped with a low-resistance material that completely covers the heel and sole (Fig. 5.1). To properly deliver the stone, a curler must have a full slider attached to the sliding foot (for right-handed players, the left foot).

There are several types of sliding materials available. The most common material, in use for years and still popular today, is Teflon. It is a good product for a beginner or someone who doesn't desire a really fast slider. Top players, however, prefer harder surfaces, which produce more speed. It is best to learn how to slide, and to develop confidence, with a material that is not overly fast. Once the basics have been perfected reasonably well, you can graduate to a quicker sliding surface. A curler's ability to slide and the

Left and right: Figure 5.1

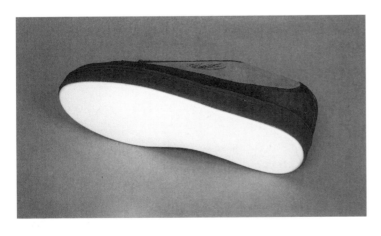
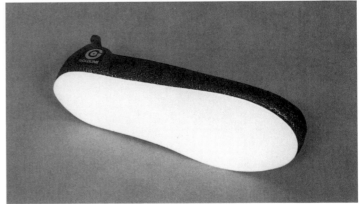

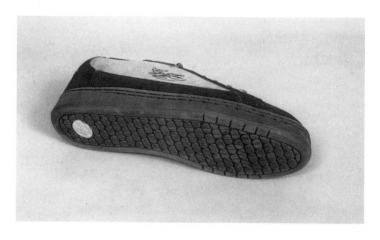 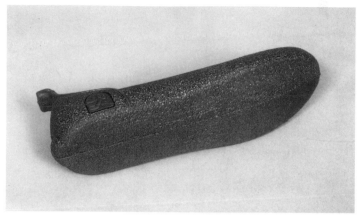

Left and right: Figure 5.2

speed of delivery should increase proportionately. Less thrust is required with a quicker sliding surface.

The sliding shoe should be worn only on the ice surface. Some sort of protection (in the form on a slip-on foam gripper) should be placed over the slider at all times that the player is not on the ice. Many curlers today use this type of gripper on both feet when sweeping. The sole of the shoe opposite the sliding sole should be completely covered with a permanent foam gripper that will offset the quickness of the sliding foot as a player moves about the ice surface (Fig. 5.2). If you are a beginner, you should cover the entire heel and sole of your sliding foot with a low-friction plastic tape before graduating to an actual curling shoe and slider.

Brushes

The brush was practically unknown in Canada and the United States as a sweeping device prior to 1980, although it has been used almost exclusively for the last fifty years in Europe (Fig. 5.3).

Calgary's Paul Gowsell was instrumental in bringing the brush into focus in North America. Gowsell stormed onto the scene in the mid-1970s and swept the world junior crown in 1976 and 1978. His teams were the first in Canadian history to enjoy huge success while using the brush, or push-broom. It caught on like wildfire. By the mid-1980s, about half of Canada's top players had switched to the brush and, by the early 1990s, the corn broom and synthetic had all but vanished. The evolution to the brush was inevitable. It lasts longer than the corn broom and is much easier to master. And, although it has never been scientifically proven, most curlers are convinced the brush works better than the broom or synthetic because it never leaves the ice surface.

Today's brushes are commonly made of three materials: hog hair, horse hair, and synthetic. The synthetic heads, usually made of nylon fabric, are becoming popular for several reasons. The synthetic brush does not shed, so there is never any possibility of a rock picking up debris from the brushing motion. It is also easier to ensure the entire surface of the brush is in full contact with the ice at all times (Fig. 5.4).

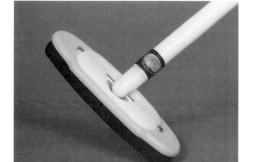

Above left and right: Figure 5.3

Left: Figure 5.4

Brush heads are available in various sizes, but the most common are 6 or 8 inches (15 or 20 cm) in width. The larger head allows the brusher to cover more surface with one stroke, but the smaller head allows greater pressure to be exerted on the ice. Brush handles also come in different sizes, but the most common are 48 inches (122 cm) in length and 1 inch (2.5 cm) in diameter. Hair brushes don't last forever, and eventually the hair will loosen and possibly shed onto the ice. It is smart to inspect a hair brush on a regular basis. Simply rub your hand across the bristles to remove any debris or frost, and then inspect the condition of the hair. Do this routinely once you finish sweeping a stone and are walking back to the throwing end for the next shot.

Brooms

Corn brooms are rare but still manufactured in small quantities for a few diehard curlers in North America (Fig. 5.5).

Gloves

The choice of gloves may seem minor but is important if you choose to throw with a glove on. If the glove is used for throwing, it needs to be tight-fitting to retain perfect feel of the stone during the delivery (Fig. 5.6). The most popular glove used today is made of deer skin and looks similar to a

Above: Figure 5.5

Top: Figure 5.6

Bottom: Figure 5.7

golf glove. Many curlers, particularly skips, have difficulty keeping their hands warm, so they wear a crafted leather mitt, shedding it just prior to delivering a stone (Fig. 5.7).

Curling Attire

There is a wide variety of fashion available today in the curling world. Most of the top North American teams wear specially designed slacks (made of a stretch material) with a matching training suit–style jacket. A golf or polo-style shirt, or a turtleneck, may be worn under the jacket. If the facility is on the cool side, some curlers resort to wearing a vest. A few women have substituted a kilt for slacks. Players in Europe favor the training suit–style garment.

Ice and Stones

Pebble

The preparation and characteristics of a sheet of ice are interesting aspects of curling. Frozen droplets on the surface of the ice, known as "pebble," are instrumental in playing the game. Without pebble, most curlers would not be able to throw a rock hard enough to reach the rings at the far end of the sheet. Rocks would also curl far too much without it. Pebble (a fine spray of water) provides thousands of frozen droplets on the ice surface that elevate the "running edge," or rim, of the stone from the surface. As a result, with less of the running edge in contact with the ice, the stone travels from end to end when a reasonable amount of force is applied, and with a playable amount of curl.

Pebble is applied with a sprinkler. The temperature of the water, how fine the spray, and the rate at which it is spread will dictate how the pebble affects the game. Ideally, the droplets of water hit the ice surface, spread slightly, and freeze. If the temperature of the water is too warm, the droplets will spread too much before freezing and flatten out. If the temperature of the water is too cold, droplets will freeze before spreading and result in the tiny "ice bumps." The application of pebble is a science that should be left in the hands of an experienced ice technician.

Fresh pebble has jagged edges, and stones have difficulty cutting through them early in a game. Later, after a number of stones have been thrown and swept, the rough edges become worn down, and more of the stone's surface comes into contact with the ice. The stone now has more surface to "bite into," and ice becomes "quicker" and with a little more curl.

Curlers in high-level competitions are usually provided ideal conditions right from the first stone. The ice technician will do one of two things once the pebble has been applied. He or she will take a cribbing, fit it around eight stones, and drag the "rock crib" from end to end a couple of times to "break down" the pebble evenly from one side of the sheet to the other. In recent years, a special blade on the ice-shaving machine has been used to provide the same pebble-breaking process and is referred to as "clipping."

Stones

Early curling rocks were nothing more than rough-shaped boulders. Circular stones with metal handles became common by 1775, and with the birth of the Royal Caledonian Club in 1838, the ultimate standardization of the size and shape of granites began to take place.

All curling stones made today weigh 42 pounds (19 kg), and both sides of the granite have concave areas referred to as cups (5 inches [13 cm] in diameter). The outer portion of the cup has a small sliding surface that is appropriately named "the rim," and it is on this very narrow rim that the stone actually travels (Fig. 5.8). The running edge, or rim, which is ideally 0.02 to 0.03 inches (5 to 7 mm) in width, is not smooth or polished like the rest of the curling stone. A stone runs on one of its running edges for approximately two years before the handle is removed, the bolt turned over, and the handle attached to the other side, allowing the rock to travel on its second running edge. The rotation of the handle must take place at regular intervals so the curler never detects any great change in the stone's reaction.

When both running edges have been worn smooth (0.03 inches [8 mm] or more), the stone must be reconditioned to restore the running edge. The reaction of a stone that is "dull," or has a worn running edge, is predictable. It will not bite in, or finish, when coming to a stop, and will drift, or float, making it difficult to judge weight. The amount of curl may be inconsistent and dependent on the temperature of the surface. The harder the surface, the less curl.

A dark gray band around the circumference of the stone is referred to as the "striking band" and is designed to absorb the shock when one stone strikes another (Fig. 5.9).

Stones are also susceptible to "pitting," the formation of irregular indentations on the running edge, where significantly large grains have fallen out. It is usually caused by the alternate freezing and melting of moisture absorbed into the running edge. This can happen early in the life of a rock if it has been stored incorrectly or placed on the ice surface while still warm.

When the running edge of a stone becomes flattened through wear or pitted from abuse, the edge must be reground, or "sharpened." This is a controversial process that has been practiced by many companies in Canada and Scotland over the past fifty years. A stone can be sharpened about three times before it is deemed unusable. Recently, a new process has been developed that can put these old stones back into service for at least another twenty years. This process involves installing an "insert." The running surface of a stone is cored out and replaced with new granite that has been preshaped, sharpened, and glued into place. The retooled stone has only one

Above: Figure 5.8

Above and right: Figure 5.9

running surface, so when it is worn out, or "pitted," the insert must be removed and a new one installed.

A freshly sharpened stone can cause a curler a fair amount of grief until it has had time to break in (a smoothing-down of the rough edges). A freshly sharpened rock has a running surface that is probably less than 0.02 inches (5 mm) in width and is very sensitive on release. The rock, turned inside slightly at release, will curl quickly; straighten it or put the handle back, and the stone will drift or fall back.

There are roughly 120,000 curling stones in use in the world today, and virtually all of them have been manufactured in Scotland from rock quarried in Scotland or Wales. One sheet of new stones costs between $12,000 and $15,000, but there have been many problems with them. The consensus is that the rock used to make all new stones in the last decade has been too soft. That's why people requiring new stones are turning to the use of inserts. A complete sheet of new inserts costs between $3,000 and $5,000.

Icemakers have often taken considerable amount of heat for the playing conditions in large arenas. That's a pity, because they usually produce a beautiful surface. The problem, more than often, is the stones.

What has changed to cause this problem? First, let's look at what puts the curl in curling. Curl is produced by the stone's running edge biting into the ice surface, or pebble, once it has had a turn applied and is on its way. Two things are going to have a bearing on exactly how this takes place: the ability of the stone to bite into the surface, and the ability of the surface to provide the stone something to bite into.

The ice surface has changed immensely over the years. Water back in Grandpa's era had impurities, or ions, that helped the rock curl. Modern technology provides de-ionized water, which saves energy since the ice plant does not have to work as hard. It also allows the icemaker to install a thinner surface, providing fingertip temperature control.

Icemakers no longer have to deal with the corn broom, which provided a great deal of influence on the curl of a stone but is no longer around. Today's ice surface is virtually sanitized. Arena surfaces have also changed dramatically. They were heavily covered in frost in the 1960s and 1970s, making for wild center/side ice variations. Power scrapers and higher temperatures on the surface have virtually eliminated frost today.

So, what impact do the stones have on this total set of circumstances? If you have a perfect stone today, it will probably work pretty well on practically every surface. A stone with a running edge between 0.02 and 0.03 inches (5 and 7 mm), without any pitting, is perfect for these conditions. It will provide an excellent reaction, except on a very hard or cold surface. The challenge for arena ice technicians, therefore, is to keep the surface as close as possible to that of a curling club. This is not always easy, since the ice technician is often fighting an air temperature of 60°F (16°C) just above the ice surface.

GAME OBJECTIVES, SCORING, AND TEAM RESPONSIBILITIES

Order of Play and Basic Responsibilities

The lead is the first player to deliver two stones, alternating with the opposing lead. Having thrown the last of his or her stones, the lead then moves up to take over brushing/sweeping duties with the number three player, and the second delivers two stones alternately with the rival second. In turn, the third (vice-skip or mate) delivers two stones that are swept by the lead and second. The fourth player, or skip, is the last to throw two stones, while a player designated by the skip, usually the third, takes over skipping duties.

The skip stands within the circles at the opposite end and directs play except when it is time to deliver his or her stones. When an end has been completed, a total of sixteen stones will have been delivered (eight per team). The basic objective is to complete each end with your stones closer to the center of the house than those of the opponent. A game is usually ten ends in length, but could be shorter, depending on the level or type of competition.

The opposing team must yield the ice to the team whose rock is being played, and not interfere in any way. The opposing skip does, however, remain behind the house in order to watch the rival stone being played so that the ice taken and action of the stone can be studied.

Curling depends upon the united efforts of all four players on the team. For a team to enjoy success, the lead's shots must be thrown with the same amount of consistency and accuracy as those of the skip. Still, it requires more experience to skip than to play lead, so novice players are advised to play lead for at least a year.

Lead

The importance of the play of the lead took an entirely new dynamic with the advent of the Free Guard Zone (FGZ) rule in the early 1990s (see Chapter 4). If the lead is able to successfully set up and come around guards with the first two rocks of the end, a team can be in control. Once it was important for the lead to be able to play a delicate draw, a quiet tap-back, or a high, hard takeout, but, with the FGZ, the primary responsibility of the lead is to play the delicate weight draws and all the soft shots. The lead and second must be excellent throwers and strong brushers, since they have the responsibility for sweeping rocks thrown by the third and skip. Effective brushing requires a great deal of strength and endurance, so quality front-enders must be in good physical condition. The ability to judge sweeping on draw shots is another trait among the best front-enders in the game.

Second

The FGZ challenges the second to follow the lead with an outstanding array of "soft" shots. If the lead can set the trend with some good "soft" shots, it is then up to the second to follow it up with two more. However, the second also needs to be a good "hitter," with the ability to execute peels, hit-and-rolls, double-takeouts, and so on, and then bounce back with perfect draw weight. It is important that the lead and second be content with their positions and understand that not everyone has the mental makeup to be a skip.

Third

The third is usually the vice-skip on most teams and, as a result, there are areas in the curling world that refer to the position as "vice-skip." The third player is often considered to be the key to the success of a competitive team, possessing the right chemistry. The third must possess the knowledge and shot-making ability of the skip, and also be an effective brusher and caller of sweeping line (the third makes the sweeping calls for the skip stones, the most important shots of the end).

Skip

The skip is the team leader who calls the play and determines where the broom, which is the thrower's target, should be placed. The skip must determine how much a particular shot will curl, which is dependent on the weight (speed of shot) thrown and the particular ice conditions. Skips must be able to execute every shot in the book under extreme pressure while maintaining poise and confidence. The skip must control the team, call the right shots, and successfully complete every shot that will give the team an advantage in determining the final outcome of the game.

Coach

Coaching in curling has become more popular in recent years with a number of competitive teams, particularly women's teams. A good coach can take a great deal of pressure off the skip by helping with the management and direction of the other three members of the team. Coaches can also become involved with developing the players' technical skills, determining and establishing gameplans, and setting short- and long-term goals for the team.

Scoring

When an end has been completed, the team with the stone closest to the center, or button, scores one point, and then counts an additional point for every stone closer to the center than the closest stone belonging to the opposing team. Stones must be in, or touching, one of the circles to be considered for scoring. The vice-skip of each team is responsible for determining and posting the score. In major competitions, game officials post the score and complete any required measurements. When the score is being determined, or a measure is taking place, all players except the vice-skips should stay out of the house until the score has been determined. The team that wins the end throws the first stone in the next end.

There are two separate types of curling scoreboards. The simplest is used on television and is commonly referred to as the "baseball"-type board. It is simple to follow: The ends are posted on the top of the scoreboard, and the score for each team is marked next to the appropriate team name and followed with a running summary at the right-hand end of the board (Fig. 5.10). This type of board is not realistic for the average curling club because it requires a large quantity of numbers. So, to make the entire process of keeping score at the club level a little easier, a different system is used.

Figure 5.10

A - Red		1														
SCORE		1	2	3	4	5	6	7	8	9	10	11	12	13	14	15
B	Yellow															

A - Red		1														
SCORE		1	2	3	4	5	6	7	8	9	10	11	12	13	14	15
B	Yellow			2												

A - Red		1														
SCORE		1	2	3	4	5	6	7	8	9	10	11	12	13	14	15
B	Yellow			2		3										

The club board system has the actual score of the game as the permanent part of the board in the center. One team name goes on the top of the score numbers, and the other below.

Let's go through a couple of hypothetical ends and mark the score for each. Team A is on the top of the board, and Team B is on the bottom. In the first end of play, Team A scores two points, so the vice-skip of Team A takes the number 1 and places it on top of the scoreboard, over the 2 (Fig. 5.11). Remember, we read the score from the middle, so after one end the score reads 2-0 for Team A. In the second end, Team B scores three points. This time the number 2, for end number two, is placed at the bottom of the board under the number 3 (Fig. 5.12). Again, reading the score from the middle of the board show that Team B leads the game 3-2.

Let's assume that, in the third end, Team B steals two points on Team A (a team steals on another when it scores points when the other team has last rock). This time the vice-skip takes the number 3 and places it under 5 on the bottom of the scoreboard. The score now reads Team A 2, Team B 5 (Fig. 5.13).

SKIP'S SIGNALS

The skip is at the distant end of the rink while the thrower is sitting in the hack about to deliver, 146 feet (45 m) away. Because of the distance between them, the skip needs to develop a system of signals to indicate to the thrower what shot is required.

The signal for a draw is for the skip to pat the ice with the broom to the spot the draw is desired, and then place the broom down as the shooting target. For a novice curler, the skip will usually hold up the hand to the side the skip wants the turn applied from. For a right-handed curler, the skip will hold up the left hand for the out-turn, and the right hand for the in-turn.

If the skip wants a stone removed, the proper signal is to tap the stone with the broom, indicating removal, and then place the broom as the thrower's target. A raise, or promotion, of a stone is signaled by tapping the rock with the broom and then holding the broom overhead, signaling by holding the hands the distance apart on the handle you want the rock promoted. A double takeout is signaled by tapping the first rock you want to strike with the broom, touching the broom to the second stone to be removed, and then placing the broom on the ice as a target.

Various types of weight (rock speed) can also be indicated to the thrower with a signal. If you want the stone removed and just passed through the circles, tap the rock for removal, and then pat the ice just behind the circles. If the stone is to be removed to the hack, tap the stone for removal, point your broom to the hack, and then place it down as the thrower's target.

These are just some examples. There are many different signals and ways for a skip to advise his or her players what is desired. It is usually up to a skip and the team to determine what is the best set of signals and then to make sure every player understands the system.

THE DELIVERY

Warm-Up

Curling at the top competitive level is no different from any other sport—it should have a physical training program. The program should involve regular and ongoing aerobic exercise for endurance, anaerobic training to develop the body's energy system for sweeping, flexibility training, and weight training. For the average curler or novice, only two aspects of the training program are important and should take place prior to the start of practice or a game.

Aerobic training might be referred to as cardiovascular, or vigorous, whole-body exercise. Top-level competitive curlers might spend thirty minutes a day on this type of training, but the recreational player needs to spend only about five minutes. This exercise will warm the body and increase blood flow to the various muscle groups. Aerobic exercises are those which are continuous and rhythmical, and provide a sustained type of movement that involves the body's large muscle groups. Activities include running on the spot, skipping, riding a stationary bike, stair-climbing, and aerobic dance.

The second, and most important, part of the warm-up segment for every curler is flexibility training or stretching. This will prevent injuries and assist the body in assuming the maximum range of body joint movement required for delivery and sweeping. Curlers at all levels need to incorporate flexibility training into the final aspect of their pregame warm-up rituals.

Stretching is easy, but there is a right way and a wrong way to do it. The right way is a relaxed, sustained approach, with your attention focused on the muscles being stretched. The wrong way (ballistic stretching) is to bounce up and down, or to stretch to the point of pain.

When you start your stretching exercises, spend between ten and thirty seconds in the easy stretch. No bouncing. Get to the point where you feel a mild tension, relax, and hold the stretch. The feeling of tension should subside as you hold the position. If it does not, ease off slightly and find a degree of tension that is comfortable. The easy stretch reduces muscular tightness and readies the tissues for the developmental stretch.

After the easy stretch, move slowly into the developmental stretch. Again, no bouncing. Move a fraction of an inch further until you again feel a mild tension, and hold for ten to thirty seconds. The tension should diminish; if not, ease off slightly. The developmental stretch fine-tunes the muscles and increases flexibility. During the stretch your breathing should be slow, rhythmic, and under control. At first, silently count the seconds for each stretch. This will ensure that you hold the proper tension for a long-enough time. After a while, you will stretch according to how it feels, without the distraction of counting.

Front Hip (Delivery Position) (Fig. 5.14)

Lower your body about halfway, into the curling delivery position, and hold the position for about twenty seconds. After the stretching feeling has diminished, lower the body into the full delivery position, and hold this developmental stretch for about twenty-five seconds. This stretch should be felt in the front hip, hamstrings, and groin. It also helps strengthen the back for the delivery.

Other areas of the body that require a similar stretching exercise are the hamstrings, groin area, spine, calves, upper body, neck, shoulders, and arms. Consult a sports physiologist or read any number of publications on the market for more detailed information.

Figure 5.14

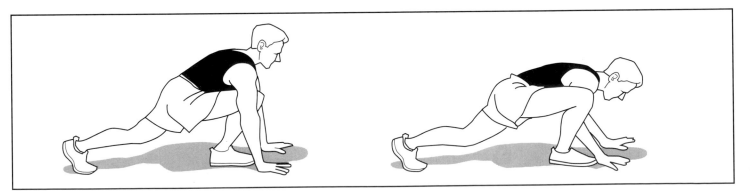

Theory of Learning the Skill

There has been a considerable amount of controversy over the past twenty-five years on how to teach an athletic skill. Some people subscribe to the whole-skill teaching approach, in which a student develops and learns a skill by watching it demonstrated in its entirety, and then tries to duplicate it. Still others believe in the part-skill teaching method, in which a student is taught the skill in segments, and after each segment has been learned and practiced, the entire skill is put together and practiced as a whole.

Because curling's skill can be broken into distinct steps, it should be taught that way. There are three separate steps to follow.

Segment No. 1

The initial movement involves the stance, hip elevation, and forward sliding motion. The emphasis is placed on the positioning of the sliding foot as the body moves forward from the hack once the weight of the body has shifted from the hack foot to the sliding foot. This is the *key* teaching element of the slide delivery. Once the weight of the body has been shifted to the sliding foot during the forward motion, the sliding foot must be under the center of the body and directly behind the stone (Fig. 5.15).

The other key element is the placement of the sliding foot on the ice. The flat-foot delivery is recommended over the tuck or toe slide. Many top curlers use the tuck delivery (a method whereby the thrower slides up on the toe and tucks the heel to the opposite thigh) with great success. However, novice or casual players looking for a simple path to success should use the flat-footed approach. It works best because both the heel and the toe remain in contact with the ice at all times, reducing both balance problems and stress on the knee. To further aid balance, the sliding-foot toe should be turned slightly outward, increasing the width of the balance point. For maximum success, it is essential to cover the heel and toe of the sliding foot with a slick, low-resistant material. A beginner can substitute a full-length slider with friction tape, covering the entire heel and sole of the sliding foot (left foot for right-handers). A slip-on slider, which covers only the toe of the shoe, is another option, but augment it with friction tape on the heel.

Segment No. 2

The second step in learning the slide delivery is to add the back-swing motion to the forward slide. The back swing is a very complex movement that requires coordination and timing. During this stage of learning, the actual delivery of the stone is still not added to the process.

Segment No. 3

The instruction aspect of this segment involves use of the stone, which means you must become knowledgeable about the grips, turns, release and line of

Figure 5.15

119

delivery. When all of these factors have been perfected, the entire delivery motion, with a stone, should be practiced repeatedly.

Ice Orientation

Before attempting any aspect of the curling delivery, a player should feel comfortable on the ice. Make sure both shoes are completely free of any foreign material. A full-length slider on the sliding foot is also essential, but make sure the opposite foot is covered with a high-resistance gripper material that will not slip on ice. Now you are ready to move to the sheet of ice.

Carefully step on the ice surface with your grip foot. Once it is firmly placed on the ice, follow with the sliding foot. With both feet on the surface, attempt to slide around slightly, being careful to keep your sliding foot under your body at all times. This is *key*. The sliding foot must remain under your body, or center of gravity. If you shift your weight away from your sliding foot, you must quickly bring your grip foot under your body. Move up and down the sheet of ice a few times to gain some confidence. Before you know it you will feel right at home.

THE STANCE

The basic positioning of the body in the hack prior to beginning the delivery is referred to as "the stance" and is the important starting point of a successful delivery. A correct and proper stance involves: (a) proper placement of the hack foot and sliding foot; (b) correct positioning of the knees, hips, and thighs; (c) correct positioning of the throwing arm and balance arm; and (d) keeping the head and upper torso in an upright, relaxed position. The key point of the stance is a position that promotes comfort and complete relaxation. No part of the body should be tight or tense. Take a deep breath and exhale just prior to beginning the delivery.

Position of the Feet

The key to balance in the stance is the positioning of the hack foot, since it supports the major portion of body weight during the back-swing and forward motion. To position the hack foot, properly step into the hack from behind it and place the ball, or center portion, of the foot firmly against the back of the hack, with the toe pointing in the direction the stone is to be delivered (Fig. 5.16). The sliding foot is positioned parallel to the hack foot and planted flat on the ice. The toe of the hack foot should be adjacent to the heel of the sliding foot, with most of the weight on the hack foot.

Figure 5.16

Position of the Head and Body

When a curler settles into the hack position, the thigh of the hack leg should be parallel to the line of delivery, the imaginary line the rock travels throughout the back and forward swing. The head should be kept comfortably erect, with the eyes trained on the target, that is, the skip's broom (Fig. 5.17).

Position of Broom Arm

Curlers throughout the world have adopted numerous approaches to positioning the non-throwing, or broom, arm during the delivery. The rules of curling allow a device other than the one you sweep with to be held by the non-throwing arm during delivery. However, it's best to use your regular sweeping device, most likely a brush. A correct or acceptable position of the broom arm is essential to maintaining proper balance throughout the delivery, at least during the first few years of curling.

Two positions are the most effective. The first has the broom and arm stretched out comfortably from the body, with the handle running toward the small of the back. If you have difficulty keeping the brush handle against the back during the forward slide, then pull the broom in toward the body and tuck it next to the elbow, with the handle again running toward the center of the back. In both cases, the head of the brush should be positioned slightly ahead of the sliding foot, with the brush hairs or brushing part of the broom facing up, and the wooden part of the head resting on the ice. The wooden head sliding along the ice will offer less resistance to your forward motion than the brush hairs when you push out of the hack (Figs. 5.18 and 5.19).

Above: Figure 5.17

Left: Figures 5.18 and 5.19

Figure 5.20

Position of Throwing Arm

The position of the throwing arm in the stance is an important aspect of a sound delivery. The throwing arm should be comfortably extended, without rigidity or tension. The stone should be placed just far enough ahead of the body for the arm to have a comfortable extension without affecting the position of the body. The arm needs to be kept in this same comfortable position during the back-swing and forward-swing motion. When the body finally comes forward from the hack, the throwing arm should have a slight bend at the elbow to maintain a comfortable extension (Fig. 5.20).

Trailing Leg and Foot

The trailing leg and foot must be extended out behind the body as far as possible during the forward slide motion. This position is initially accomplished by extending the trailing leg out behind you as far as possible during the leg-drive phase of the forward motion, allowing the toe of the hack foot to be flipped back against the hack. This flipping motion of the toe allows for a complete extension of the trailing leg without the leg touching any portion of the ice. The flipping motion will have the trailing toe placed in one of three positions: (1) turned over and inside toward the body; (2) straight up and down; or (3) slightly turned to the outside but with only the toe in contact with the ice (Figs. 5.21, 5.22, and 5.23).

Figure 5.21   Figure 5.22   Figure 5.23

Segment No. 1

If you plan to learn the curling delivery in three separate segments, it is time to go to the ice and perfect this segment. Start by standing in the hack with your hack foot. Take your broom, grip it close to the head, and extend it about 2 feet (60 cm) in front of your hack foot, with the tip of the handle touching the ice. Raise the broom about a foot above the ice and gently tap down on the ice so it makes a slight mark about 2 feet in front of your hack foot.

Assume the balanced stance in the hack, as outlined. When you are comfortable, and using the strength of both legs, slowly begin to elevate the hips while keeping the position of the upper body constant. When the legs have been elevated to a point that would normally be assumed if a back swing had taken place and the forward swing was about to begin, move the sliding foot toward the small mark you placed on the ice with the broom handle. When the sliding foot is covering the mark, reach forward with the sliding foot and, at the same time, push the hack foot hard against the back of the hack. As this motion is completed and the weight shifts from the hack foot to the sliding foot, you will begin to slide forward from the hack.

As you are reaching forward with the sliding foot, begin to turn the toe of the sliding foot out slightly (if possible). This will accomplish two things: it will increase the actual width of your sliding surface, making balance easier,

Figure 5.24

Figure 5.25

Figure 5.26

and it will release the knee of the sliding leg to the outside, allowing the body to naturally sink forward at the release point of the delivery. The upper body should be in the same upright position as you leave the hack that it held in the stance. The body should be lowered gradually during the forward slide, reaching its lowest position shortly after the stone has been released. You should begin this exercise using a minimal amount of forward thrust, and gradually increase the drive as your balance improves.

The key point in this drill is balance. It can be accomplished only if the sliding foot is positioned under the center of the body and remains in that groove throughout the entire slide (Figs. 5.24, 5.25, and 5.26).

Forward Press, and Back and Forward Swing

The second step to the slide delivery adds the forward press, back swing, and forward swing to the skill.

There are two approaches to consider in the back swing. For years curlers were taught to pick the stone up off the ice during the back swing. Today, however, a popular method is to leave the stone on the ice (no back-swing or rock-swing delivery).

In keeping with the part-skill instruction approach, the back-swing motion is Segment No. 2; as a result, the stone is not involved with the motion.

Forward Press

The forward press is a slight forward motion of rock and body that serves as a starting point for the back swing. The forward press is an optional motion. Don't exaggerate this motion because doing so could pull your body off line.

Back Swing

The back-swing motion starts as the stone is slowly drawn back and both legs begin to elevate the body from the hips. As the rock begins to be swung off the ice, most of the body's weight begins to shift to the hack leg. It will remain centered over the hack foot and leg during the entire back swing until weight transfer takes place from the hack foot to the sliding foot at the beginning of the forward slide. The position of the upper body varies only slightly during the entire motion. The hack leg is the only part of the body to elevate.

The movement and timing of the sliding foot are critical to the back-swing delivery. When the stone begins to leave the ice and move into an arc, the sliding foot begins a backward motion at the same time. The sliding foot should move straight back from the hack, but there could be slight individual variations. The weight of the stone, as it begins to leave the ice, tends to cause an inward rotation of the hack hip, but the backward movement of the sliding foot acts as a counter-balance and keeps the upper body square. The swing of the stone should never exceed the height of the

Clockwise from bottom left:
Figure 5.27, Figure 5.28, Figure 5.29, and Figure 5.30

knee, and the stone should reach the top of its pendulum at the same time the sliding foot reaches its farthest point back. Most of the sliding foot surface should remain in contact with the ice during the entire back-swing motion.

Forward Swing

When all of the timing factors are complete, there should be a natural pause when the stone reaches the top of the swing. Now the weight of the stone begins the forward motion, accelerated by the arm, and continues until the stone touches the ice in the forward motion. The amount of acceleration is proportionate to the desired speed, or weight, of the shot. When the forward motion begins, it is important for the sliding foot to delay. The stone must precede the sliding foot in the forward motion (Figs. 5.27, 5.28, 5.29, and 5.30).

Figure 5.31

Forward Movement of the Sliding Foot

The most important element in delivering a stone correctly is the movement of the sliding foot from the top of the swing until the weight shifts from the hack foot to the sliding foot in the forward motion. When the stone begins to move forward, at the top of the swing, the sliding foot must be deliberately delayed so the stone can be extended ahead of the sliding foot. Just as the stone touches down, the sliding foot begins to move forward and in behind the stone. During the time that the extension of the sliding foot and leg is taking place, the weight of the body is shifted from the hack leg to the sliding leg. As this shift takes place, the hack leg drives against the back of the hack and pushes, or drives, as hard as necessary to accelerate the body.

When the weight shift has been completed, the sliding foot should be 12 to 24 inches (30 to 60 cm) directly behind the stone. It is also important to move the sliding foot gradually behind the stone. This will prevent the curler from taking the sliding foot laterally across the line of delivery (the imaginary line the stone travels on toward the skip's broom at the far end), which is the common cause of a drift (sideways motion) in the delivery (Fig. 5.31).

Position of Upper Body

During the start of the forward-slide motion, it is important to keep the upper body in the same position as in the stance. During the forward slide and through to the completion of the delivery, the upper body gradually sinks in behind the stone, with the lowest point and fullest extension taking place a few inches behind the final release (Figs. 5.32 and 5.33).

Figure 5.32

Figure 5.33

No-Back-Swing Delivery

Many of today's top players use some form of the no-back-swing delivery, including two-time Brier champion Kevin Martin of Edmonton and world champion Wayne Middaugh of Toronto. Without question, the smooth delivery motion, with the stone never leaving the ice, is the most desirable. There's no need to correct the line of the stone as it moves around the leg, in either the back or the forward motion. And no acceleration is required from the strength of the arm or the thrust of the leg.

The key to the no-back-swing delivery is a "falling motion" required during the forward motion of the delivery to give the stone its momentum. This seems to be accomplished by drawing the center of gravity straight back during the back swing, making sure the hack leg extends the body up to a

Figure 5.34

point where the right arm remains straight and the right shoulder is directly over the stone at the top of the backward motion. The necessary forward momentum comes from the center of gravity being on the right shoulder as the forward motion begins (Fig. 5.34).

The initial motion for a no-back-swing delivery differs little from a normal back swing. Again, the motion starts with a forward press, the legs start to elevate the hips, and the stone is drawn back in a straight line to the hack foot. When the stone reaches its farthest point back, the sliding foot is moved behind the body. When this point has been reached, it is essential that the body is elevated from the hips so that the right shoulder is directly over the stone and the throwing arm fully extended.

From this point the forward motion begins by the weight of the body falling forward onto the stone. The forward movement of the sliding foot is delayed for a greater period of time than with the regular back-swing delivery. When the sliding foot does make its forward move, it happens much quicker than with the back-swing delivery. This delay is necessary so the final drive of the hack leg will come as late as possible during the forward motion. This means the final thrust of the hack leg will be more horizontal than vertical, which will provide optimum drive (Figs. 5.35, 5.36, and 5.37).

Another approach to the no-back-swing delivery has been introduced recently. It uses a slightly different method of developing momentum. During the initial motion, the hips remain low, with the hips and the sliding foot reaching back (about 24 inches [60 cm]) to a position whereby the majority of body weight is shifted to the sliding foot. This shift is possible because the

Figures 5.35, 5.36, and 5.37

entire surface of the sliding foot stays in contact with the ice at all times. When you have reached the farthest point back, prior to starting the forward motion, the shoulder of the throwing arm is not over the stone because the hips have not been elevated high enough for this to happen. Instead, the shoulders are back over the hack foot and the throwing arm is extended forward on an angle.

Figures 5.38, 5.39, and 5.40

The forward motion starts by shifting the center of gravity from the sliding foot to the hack foot. This has the effect of thrusting the weight of the body forward in a "leaping" motion. When this shift has taken place, the weight of the body has again been shifted to the sliding foot, which is behind the stone, and the final thrust of the body is completed by the push of the hack leg to full extension. Again, this is a slightly different method than the "falling on stone" tactic in the no-back-swing delivery (Figs. 5.38, 5.39, and 5.40).

Segment No. 2

The second stage of learning the delivery in segments adds a back swing, or back motion, to the initial slide but still omits use of a stone.

Spend a few minutes reviewing Segment No.1 and then start to concentrate on Segment No. 2. The key point to be aware of in this segment is the movement of the sliding foot. When you have completed the forward press, the stone is drawn back. During this phase of the delivery, both feet are used to elevate the body so the sliding foot remains stationary. If the back-swing delivery is utilized, the sliding foot begins to move back once the stone starts to leave the ice. With the no-back-swing delivery, the sliding foot starts back once the stone has been drawn back to the hack foot. Prior to the start of the forward motion, the sliding foot reaches its farthest point back behind the body. The forward motion starts, in the case of the back-swing delivery, with the rock being swung forward; in the case of no back swing, the body begins to fall forward onto the stone, or the weight starts to shift from the sliding foot to the hack foot. In both cases, the sliding foot is delayed at its position behind the body. When the stone is well out and ahead of the body, the sliding foot is moved forward and in behind the stone.

Figures 5.41, 5.42, 5.43, and 5.44

A cadence can be used to assist with the correct order of movements. The cadence is stone/foot/stone/foot. Initially, the stone moves back, the foot is delayed, and then the foot moves back. During the forward motion, the stone is the first to move forward, and then the foot.

GRIPS, TURNS, AND RELEASE

There are a few other items to be considered prior to advancing to the actual grip and delivery of the stone. They include cleaning the stone, the line of delivery, and the follow-through.

Cleaning the Stone

To ensure there is nothing lodged on the running edge of the stone, the rim should be cleaned. Flip the stone over and clean the running edge with a broom or brush. Run your fingers along the running edge as a final check for any small pieces of grit. When the cleaning has been completed, pull the stone aside and clean the entire area in front of the hack before turning the stone back onto its rim (Figs. 5.41, 5.42, 5.43, and 5.44).

Many curlers spin the stone a number of times on the ice prior to delivery, a practice first started by former world champion Russ Howard. The theory is that spinning the stone will tend to fill any "pitting" the stone might have with ice, thus reducing the potential impact on the path of the stone as it travels from end to end.

Line of Delivery

An important but often overlooked factor is the position and alignment of the stone and body in accordance with the skip's broom at the distant end. This is relatively simple when the skip holds the broom on the center line because the line of delivery, or imaginary line, is the center line. So, in the hack position, the center line bisects the stone, and the body sits parallel to the center line. When the weight transfer has been completed in the forward-slide motion, the sliding foot will move straight down the center line, which will now bisect the entire body.

However, the skip's broom doesn't always stay on the center line. As it moves across the sheet and side to side, the body and stone must be adjusted accordingly to keep the line of delivery straight.

Let's consider how the stone and body might be adjusted when the skip moves the broom to the outside edge of the 12-foot circle to the thrower's right. At this point, the center line should have slightly less than one-third to the left of it and two-thirds to the right of it. The entire body is adjusted again to the thrower's left so the body remains parallel to the line of delivery.

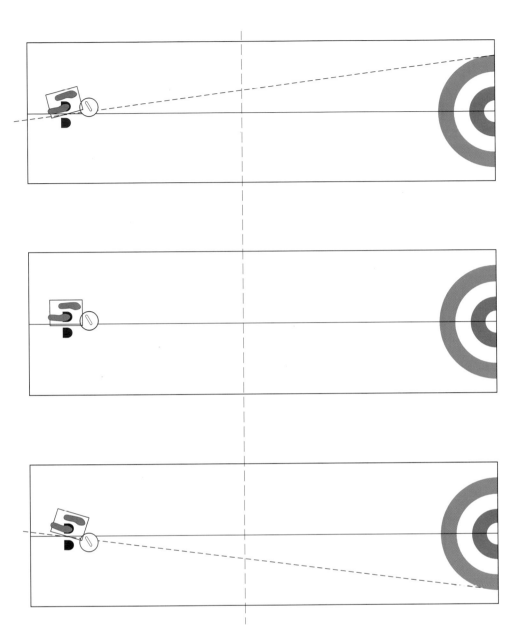

Figure 5.45

As the skip moves the broom back toward center, the adjustment is reduced until the broom is again positioned at the center of the house and the center line is bisecting the stone as the player sits in the hack. The same adjustment and principles apply if the broom is moved to the thrower's right until it touches the outside edge of the 12-foot circle. At this point, the center line should have slightly less than one-third to the right of it and two-thirds to the left of it. There are a few rare shots in curling, to the wide outside, that you would start as you sit in the hack with less than one-third of the stone touching the center line (Fig. 5.45).

Position of Throwing Arm

When the body comes forward from the hack during the forward slide, the upper torso remains in relatively the same position it held in the stance. During the initial stage of the forward slide, the throwing arm might be

fairly straight, particularly in the no-back-swing delivery. However, as the body comes forward from the hack, there should be a slight bend at the elbow, or a relaxed position in the throwing arm. The arm needs to be kept in this position until just prior to release so the wrist can be kept high through completion of the release motion. The ability to have some extension left in the throwing arm at release also plays a major role in developing a last-second correction in the weight control of the stone (Figs. 5.46 and 5.47).

Point of Release

The point of release and manner of release are probably the most critical factors in the delivery. The release point can vary on any shot by adjusting the amount of momentum applied to the forward slide. It is best to release every shot, takeout or draw, in the same general area, with a maximum of about a 3- to 4-foot (1- to 1.2-m) variation. This can be accomplished by adjusting the amount of forward momentum from the hack for either the draw or the takeout.

Follow-Through

A proper follow-through motion involves keeping the eyes on the skip's broom, the throwing arm extended forward and the slide continuing behind the released stone. A potentially good shot can be spoiled by making any sudden movements at release, like attempting to stand quickly, dropping your hand to the ice to aid in balance, or pulling your hand away from the stone to prevent a hog-line foul (Figs. 5.48 and 5.49).

The In-Turn Grip

Left: Figure 5.48

Right: Figure 5.49

A novice should grip the handle of the stone firmly, but not too hard. The index and two middle fingers are placed near the front part of the handle, with the thumb pressed firmly against the side of the handle to provide grip control. The V formed between the thumb and the index finger should point to the opposite shoulder. The handle should rest comfortably on the second joint of the last three fingers. The wrist must be kept in a high position through to the final release of the stone. This enables a rotation to be applied to the stone by a turn of the wrist rather than a flip of the fingers.

The in-turn can be acceptably gripped in one of two positions: with the handle straight, or with a 20- to 30-degree counter-rotated handle to the turn. The 20- to 30-degree counter-position is recommended for novice players. Imagine the curling rock as the face of a clock. The end of the handle pointing back to you would be in the 6-o'clock position. Rotate the handle 20 to 30 degrees in a counter-clockwise direction, taking the handle somewhere between 4- and 5-o'clock position. The handle position must be maintained during the back swing and forward motion through to the point of release. In a space of between 2 and 3 feet (60 and 90 cm) prior to release, the in-turn is applied to the stone with a distinct and inward rotation of the wrist, hand, and forearm. This motion should find the hand in the handshake position, and behind the stone a few moments after release. The handshake position is used as a point of reference, allowing the stone to be released in exactly the same manner on every shot. For a right-handed player, the in-turn starts the stone rotating in a clockwise direction. It might help you to remember that the in-turn is applied by an inward rotation of the wrist (Figs. 5.50, 5.51, and 5.52).

The Out-Turn Grip

The same reference point at release (the handshake position) is recommended for the in-turn and the out-turn. Start again in the hack with the a straight handle. This time rotate the handle about 30 degrees in a clockwise direction to about 8 o'clock. This adjustment must be maintained during the entire back swing and forward motion until just prior to the point of release. About 2 to 3 feet (60 to 90 cm) prior to the point of release, the out-turn is applied to the stone by a distinct rotation of the wrist and forearm to the handshake position. It is important that the throwing-arm wrist stay high through the entire process prior to release and the arm maintain a slight bend at the elbow (Figs. 5.53, 5.54, and 5.55).

Top left: Figure 5.50

Top right: Figure 5.51

Bottom left: Figure 5.52

Segment No. 3

Now it is time to attempt the complete delivery with the stone. But first it is advisable to develop a feel for the motion required to properly apply both turns. To do this you need a partner. Position yourself on one sheet divider with your partner facing you across the width of the ice from the other divider. Get into the hack position with the back of your hack foot on the divider. Take a stone by the handle and properly apply the in-turn grip. Next perform the press, slide the stone back, and rotate the handle for the in-turn release by pushing it across the sheet to your partner. Practice handle adjustments and release of the in-turn while pushing a stone back and forth with your partner for about ten minutes. Then repeat the drill with the out-turn handle adjustment, release, and handshake follow-through.

Next you should work on throwing the stone from the hack to the first hog line, again with the help of a partner. Have your partner hold the broom

down the center line so your line of delivery is straight down the middle of
the sheet. Practice both turns, and focus on reaching your sliding foot straight
down the line of delivery as you come forward from the hack.

After you begin to feel some level of comfort, have the broom holder at
the hog line place the broom at various points within the maximum line of
delivery adjustments.

Figures 5.53, 5.54, and 5.55

Handle Rotation

A consistently delivered stone with a positive release applied to its handle
should take two to three complete revolutions from hack to distant house. A
stone released in this manner will react nearly the same every time with little
chance of it losing its turn. It is also desirable for a stone to travel about 20
to 30 feet (6 to 9 m) from the point of delivery before it begins to curl. This
makes sweeping more of a factor in holding the line of a stone. A stone with
fewer than one and one half turns will not react consistently and will likely
curl more than a positively released stone. It can also lose its turn easily. A
spinning type of release is acceptable if takeouts are being played because
the stone will run very straight. However, it becomes very difficult to execute
any sort of come-around shot since the stone will not curl as desired.

Weight Control

By now you have developed a reasonable understanding of the slide delivery and
how to correctly release the stone. You are now ready to develop the weight, or
speed, of the stone delivered. A consistent point of release and proper follow-
through motion will also contribute to the development of weight-control skills.
Weight control is learned by repetition and developing a feel for the desired speed.
This can be done by attempting to deliver about ten stones to the same point on
the ice, starting at a point about ten feet inside the far hog line. This might be done
in groupings of four, with a series of ten inside the far hog, ten at the front of the
12-foot circle, twelve at the back of the 12-foot circle, and twelve to the back board.

A stopwatch will help you with weight control when you actually start playing the game. Time can be measured in two ways. Start the watch when the leading edge of the stone touches the first hog line and stop it when it comes to rest. This should take twenty-four seconds on regular ice conditions in most facilities in Canada. If the ice keens up a little, that might move to twenty-five or twenty-six seconds. If the pebble flattens out and the ice gets a little tougher, the speed might reduce to twenty-one or twenty-two seconds. In some parts of the world, time is measured only between the hog lines. The average time under this system is about fourteen seconds.

SWEEPING

Purpose of Sweeping

There have been many theories over the years regarding the purpose of sweeping. When the sport originated hundreds of years ago, sweeping was initially necessary to clear snow from the path of the stone as it traveled from end to end. In time, the purpose of sweeping has evolved and today might be considered to do the following:

- cause a slight melting effect on the pebble and, thus, temporarily create a film of moisture, making is easier for the stone to advance;

- smooth the pebble and remove frost that reduces the friction between the stone and the ice;

- clean the ice and remove debris in the path of the stone.

It is obvious that sweeping effectiveness is proportional to the number of strokes and the strength behind the sweeping motion. Effective sweeping reduces friction in the path of the stone and, as a result, helps maintain its momentum longer—an important concept. Many curlers believe sweeping helps increase the speed of the stone, but that's simply impossible. By reducing friction in the path of the stone, it is possible to keep it in motion longer and help it travel farther. A stone might also be swept if it is curling too much, thus the common term "keep it straight."

Sweeping helps maintain the momentum of the stone longer, meaning it will arrive at the distant end sooner. Let's consider two stationary points on the ice—points A and B. An unswept stone will pass from point A to point B in a certain time interval. A swept stone, however, will pass between points A and B in less time. The amount a stone will curl between two points on the ice is also affected by the time it is in motion between those two points. So, if a stone is swept between the points, the time it is in motion will be reduced; the stone has less time to curl, and thus slides straighter.

Sweeping Effectiveness

Effective sweeping requires strength, endurance, proper techniques, and repetition. Many top curlers spend hours developing endurance and strength through specially designed programs. A recreational player needs to first perfect the proper techniques. It is important initially for you to learn a smooth, rhythmic stroke that can be applied with a reasonable amount of speed and pressure. For our purposes, we will keep the brushing stroke simple and teach you to develop a motion that keeps the path of the brush working perpendicular to the path of the stone (many competitive curlers, however, feel the most effective motion is developed by having the head of the brush moving roughly in the same direction the stone is traveling).

Brushing

Since 1980, the brush, or push-broom, has dominated the curling scene in North America. Corn brooms are rarely, if ever, used to sweep. It has been an interesting transition because in the mid-1970s brushes were as scarce in North American curling as corn brooms are today.

Since the brush is still relatively new to the North American game, it isn't surprising to see variety in brushing techniques. Many of the brushing variations have been developed by competitive curlers who have perfected their particular technique. However, we'll keep brushing to the basics and make it relatively easy for the novice to learn. This technique permits the curler to easily assume a balanced position but does not allow for full body weight to be applied to the brush head.

Stance and Grip

The side of the rock you sweep from is determined by your sliding foot. If your slider is on the left foot, then you sweep from the left side of the stone. You should begin with your feet about shoulder-width apart, and your knees slightly bent. The front foot (sliding foot) should be turned out slightly, which will turn the hips out at about an angle of 45 degrees. Position your upper body slightly forward so the weight of the body is centered on the sliding foot (Figs. 5.56 and 5.57).

Position the brush across the front of your body so that it drops down in front of your sliding foot. If you are on the left side of the path of the stone, grip the brush about halfway to two-thirds down the shaft with your right hand. Place your left hand, palm up, in a comfortable position about 2 feet (60 cm) from the end of the handle. Pull the elbow of your left hand (top hand on broom) in close to your body to help hold the broom steady. Then, simply lean forward onto your sliding foot. This will result in you pressing

down with both hands on the handle and, in turn, transferring pressure to the brush head. The angle between the ice and the brush handle should be about 60 degrees for the average brusher. The stroke of the brush should be kept short and cover the entire path of the stone.

Footwork for Brushing

When waiting to sweep a stone, stand well to the side and position yourself at approximately the back line. Do not position yourself in a spot that would interfere with the thrower who is about to deliver the stone. As the thrower begins the back-swing motion, start to move forward slightly ahead of the player delivering the stone, so you might begin sweeping when the stone is released.

The type of footwork used for this basic brushing technique is referred to as the "push–glide" method. To complete this procedure effectively you must have a good gripper on your back, or right foot, and a slider on your left, or sliding foot. The knees are slightly bent and the front foot slightly open. The body's center of gravity is positioned over the sliding foot at all times. The

gripper foot pushes the body with a scissor-type motion as you move down the ice. The grip foot comes up to the sliding foot and pushes back. When the back leg is extended, it comes forward and plants for the next push.

When you first attempt a brushing motion, do it from a stationary position until you get a feel for the motion required. Once you have built up some confidence, practice sweeping down the sheet utilizing the push–glide motion. Sweep from end to end without a stone, keeping your sweeping motion down the center line. When you feeling comfortable with the basic sweeping techniques in motion have a partner throw a stone as you attempt to sweep it from end to end.

Alternate Footwork

If you want to brush on the opposite side of the stone, or use a brushing method that applies more force to the brushing motion, the use of a gripper on each foot is recommended. The body is again positioned at about 45 degrees to the path of the stone. As you move down the ice, the center of gravity shifts from one foot to the other, with the weight at any given time centered on the foot that is leading the body. This method of footwork also allows greater pressure to be applied to the brush head as you move down the ice (Figs. 5.58 and 5.59).

Brushing with a Partner

It was once normal for both sweepers to sweep from the same side of the stone. Today, however, it has become more common for sweepers to be on each side of the stone. Beginners should first master the push–glide footwork, which will make it necessary for both sweepers to be positioned on the same side of the stone. As you become more proficient as a sweeper, you will want to work on developing your skill from both sides of the stone.

The sweeper next to the stone is referred to as the "inside," or "lead," sweeper. The lead sweeper has the responsibility of judging the weight, or speed of the stone, and must decide on whether or not to sweep the stone for weight. To do this effectively, the inside sweeper must constantly scan the distance from the stone to the final destination.

Figure 5.60

If both sweepers are positioned on the same side, it is important for the inside sweeper to be positioned close to the stone. This allows the outside, or front, sweeper to move in close to the inside sweeper without causing a collision. The outside sweeper must reach slightly farther with the arms in order to sweep across the path of the stone. The outside sweeper must watch the path of the stone and be aware of the inside sweeper's position since the inside sweeper is busy judging the stone. The outside sweeper can assist in the judging of the rock speed by offering suggestions to the inside sweeper, who remains in charge of the sweeping decision for weight (Fig. 5.60).

If the two sweepers are on opposite sides of the stone, the judging responsibility still rests with the lead sweeper. However, the positioning of the two sweepers becomes an independent decision (Fig. 5.61).

Sweeping with a Corn Broom

Few curlers today sweep with the corn broom. It remains a curiosity, but few people fully appreciate the skill required to operate a corn broom correctly. The use of the corn broom dropped off in the late 1970s and early 1980s in favor of the brush because of cost, straw debris left on the ice, and the extra energy needed to use it. The way the game is played today—particularly under arena conditions—makes the corn broom undesirable.

Figure 5.61

Strategy

What type of game do you want to play. Aggressive? Defensive? There is a definite terminology associated with defining the different types of play in curling. The words "offensive" and "aggressive" usually refer to a strategy a team might employ to score more than a single in an end with last rock, or steal at least one point without last rock (a "steal" is scoring when the opponent has last stone). Other terms associated with aggressive play include "delicate," "finesse," and "fine," indicating the various types of shots. This style of play is often referred to as the "draw game" but has also been termed "risky" or "complicated." Defensive play is a cautious and simplistic approach that uses a "takeout game," which leaves few rocks in play.

BASIC STRATEGY

Curling strategy is a tough subject to teach, simply because of the nature of the game. Teams find themselves in all sorts of situations during the course of a game. Basic strategy is in how they deal with those situations. It could be the ability to grasp the conditions and changes in the ice surface quicker than the opponent, or playing to another team's weakness (detecting a delivery flaw and taking advantage of it), or knowing how and when to play a conservative takeout type of game versus an aggressive draw style.

Strategy is also knowing how to execute different types of shots, and the type of weight desired for each of them. Every member of a team must develop the sense of what he or she is doing with every type of shot for a team to have success. A good skip will always ask other members of the team to play shots they execute the best, and perhaps lure the opponent into playing their style of game.

In many curling games it often comes down to what is referred to as "last-rock advantage." The team with last-rock advantage in an end is usually considered to be in control. Last-rock advantage is so important that it is common practice for a skip to throw his or her last rock of an end through the rings to blank the end (no points). That way the skip retains last-rock advantage in the next end and has the possibility of scoring two or more points. (The winner of a particular end throws the first rock in the next end. If the end is blanked the throwing order of the previous end is followed.)

The Free Guard Zone (FGZ) has changed curling strategy at all levels so much that there is no longer a standard approach to curling that might be used at certain stages of the game. However, the following principles are still generally followed by average teams in the sport:

1. In the early ends of the game, both teams are likely to throw the first stone in the rings, and play cautiously until the ice conditions and the play of the opponent is a little more familiar.

2. After a few ends, the skip will usually take a few more chances and attempt to score more than one point when in possession of the last rock. Without it, the skip might still play cautiously.

3. A skip up by three or more points will generally play defensively and attempt to limit the opponent to one point, or steal more points and pad the lead.

4. A skip losing by two or more will probably play a very offensive style and gamble every end in an attempt to get back in the game.

EVOLUTION OF THE FREE GUARD ZONE (FGZ)

Curling was originally played outdoors on a natural ice surface that was exposed to all the elements. The stone was delivered from a crampit, and sweeping was used to keep snow from the path of the stone. Stones were crude and inconsistent. At this stage of the game's development, simply drawing a stone into the house was no easy feat. And to remove a stone from the circles was, at times, virtually impossible.

It's hard to believe, but in some corners of the world curling still takes place under these crude conditions. Players in curling's backwaters often play on an ice surface previously used for hockey, and throw stones flawed with pits and many other irregularities. However, the sport has evolved to a much higher level in North America and some parts of Europe.

The late 1940s and early 1950s brought a number of innovations to the sport. Matched stones and the slide delivery are two examples. These changed the game drastically in the curling-club setting, but there were still problems when the game moved into big arenas during the 1960s and early 1970s. It wasn't until the dawn of the 1980s that a number of developments changed the game at the top competitive level.

The ice conditions became more refined as ice technicians learned what was required to keep a consistent surface from side to side, and from game to game, in an arena. The corn broom was gradually displaced by the brush. And the slide delivery grew longer and faster with the relaxation of the old hog-line rule for delivery.

But along with these adjustments came a downside. Arena ice surfaces became straighter, with less curl, partly due to the use of de-ionized water and the elimination of corn-broom chaff. Stones with dull or wide running edges were often used, and they refused to curl much on the hard ice surfaces required in an arena setting.

Suddenly, top-caliber teams became more proficient at reading the ice. Games with scores of 2-1 and 2-0 were not uncommon. Pat Ryan's Edmonton team of the 1980s was a prime example. They were so proficient at peeling guards that a single-point lead in the second end was often enough to carry them to victory. The game was being reduced to an unappetizing pulp, decided as early as the coin flip.

Something needed to be done, so a number of top curlers looked for ways to inject some excitement back into the game—or to put the "curl" back into curling. One of the concepts, born of the late 1980s, was the brainchild of 1987 and 1993 world champion Russ Howard of Canada. His idea was simple: Lead players would no longer be allowed to play takeouts. This rule had two immediate positives: it ensured there would be rocks in play and it eliminated the possibility of a team nursing a lead to the finish line by simply peeling everything in sight.

Around the same time, a group in Moncton, New Brunswick, was organizing a major bonspiel in recognition of the city's 100th anniversary. The Moncton 100 was billed the largest cashspiel in history, with a total purse of $250,000. The bonspiel committee liked Howard's idea and immediately adopted it. The Moncton Rule was born.

The Moncton Rule

1. Leads are not permitted to remove opposition stones from play.

2. Leads can move a stone to a different position in the playing area but if an opponent's stationary stone is hit, peeled, or otherwise bumped out of the playing area, the opposition stone will be replaced to its original position, and the shooter removed.

3. Leads can throw each of their stones through the house or remove stones belonging to their own team.

The results of the Moncton Rule were dramatic. Suddenly games became high-scoring shootouts. The wide-open style opened the door to all manner of come-from-behind heroics. Teams trailing 4-1 after five ends were no longer out of it, although it also led to the possibility of 10-1 blowout games.

Leads became all-important. They could quickly make or break a team on their abilities to play, and consistently lead to the quiet come-around draws and tap-backs.

But the Moncton Rule also posed a dilemma. Did curling really want a situation where the lead never had the opportunity to throw a takeout or a peel?

The Four-Rock Rule

The debate regarding the role of the lead continued long after the Moncton 100 became part of curling history. Competitive players and fans felt the Moncton Rule would drastically change the role and abilities of the four players on a team if it was used for national and international championships. It was argued that leads throwing only draws would feel stifled and limited as curlers.

A solution was suggested: The lead would be allowed to take out stones in the rings only. The idea was used in a bonspiel in Lausanne, Switzerland, in the fall of 1990. Two well-known European curlers, David Smith of Scotland and Eigil Ramsfjell of Norway, liked this variation of the rule. In fact, Ramsfjell liked it so much he managed to convince the Norwegian Curling Association to submit it as a proposal to the semi-annual meeting of the World Curling Federation at Lillehammer, Norway, in December 1990.

To the surprise of many—mainly North Americans—the WCF accepted the proposal and agreed to adopt this modification of the Moncton 100 for all world championship play, starting with the 1992 Winter Olympics in Albertville, France, where curling was included as a demonstration sport. The WCF labeled the area in front of the circles "the Free Guard Zone" and the rule is now universally known as "the Four-Rock Rule." It reads:

1. The area between the hog line and the tee line, excluding the house, shall be the Free Guard Zone.

2. No stone lying within this zone may be removed from play by the opposition until the first four stones played in any end have come to rest. Any stone removed from play by the opposition under those circumstances shall immediately be replaced where it previously lay, and the offending stone removed from play. Any other stone, the position of which changed as a consequence of this infraction, shall likewise be replaced where it previously lay. All stones shall be replaced to the satisfaction of the skip of the non-offending team.

3. For any stone lying in the house, the normal rules of play shall apply at all times. Notwithstanding, the rules of play number 4 (9), (WCF) a stone may be measured with an instrument by an umpire to determine whether or not it is in the house. A stone touching the Free Guard Zone and the house shall be considered in the house.

The Three-Rock Rule

When the WCF adopted the Four-Rock Rule, the Canadian Curling Association considered the matter at its policy meetings, went back to the WCF, and asked the world body to put the matter on a two-year review before acceptance. The WCF refused.

The CCA felt it was necessary to proceed with caution and established a two-year review, before making a decision on Canadian championship play in June 1993. It was easier for Europeans and others outside Canada to adopt the new rule because they dealt, in the main, with competitive curlers. Canada, on the other hand, has to deal with more recreational curlers than the rest of the curling world combined.

In the meantime, a number of top players at Canada's competitive level began to consider the merits of the Four-Rock Rule. There were two major concerns:

- The leads can never throw a peel and, for the most part, seldom a normal weight takeout. (Leads were more vocal on this one.)

- Since leads are never allowed to throw a peel, most of the game's strategy revolved around the 4-foot circle and seldom does any strategy develop to the side of the sheet. One of the game's great strategies, use of the corner guard, was being tossed aside, along with use of the outside portion of the ice.

These concerns lead a number of curlers to experiment with variations of the rule. One of the innovators was Dave Merklinger of Ottawa, who felt concerns about the rule would be dashed if the number of stones in the FGZ was reduced to three. The slight modification accomplished three things:

- The leads, on occasion, could throw a peel shot.

- With three rocks rather than four, the center-ice area did not become instant gridlock. Corner guards could still be a big part of the game, and the side of the ice could receive as much play as the center.

- The original concern of getting more rocks in play and discouraging peel-and-run strategy was accomplished.

The CCA made the decision in June 1993 to adopt the Three-Rock Rule, as follows:

1. The area between the hog line and the tee line, excluding the house, shall be the Free Guard Zone. A stone which comes to rest outside the rings, but touching the tee line, is not in the Free Guard Zone.

2. Any stone located within the Free Guard Zone shall not be removed from play until the delivery of the fourth stone of the end. This includes your

own team's stones. **Penalty**: If a stone in the Free Guard Zone is removed from play prior to the delivery of the fourth stone of the end, the non-offending team should request the game clock be stopped and may:

a) If it is to the advantage of the non-offending team, and with the approval of the supervisor or head official, waive the Free Guard Zone penalty and continue;

b) Remove the delivered stone from play and replace all displaced stationary stones to their original position. If the teams cannot agree, the official will replace all displaced stones to their original position.

3. If, in the delivery of the third stone of the end, a stone not in the FGZ is hit initially and, as a result, a stone in the FGZ is removed from play, the non-offending team should request the game clock stopped and may:

a) If it is to the advantage of the non-offending team, and with the approval of the official, waive the Free Guard Zone penalty and continue to play as if there had not been an infraction;

b) Remove the delivered stone from play and replace the stone removed from the Free Guard Zone to its original position. The stone that was initially hit will remain where it finally comes to rest. If the teams cannot agree, the official will replace the stone removed from the Free Guard Zone to its original position.

4. After delivery of each of the first three stones of an end, it is the responsibility of the throwing-team skip to ensure agreement with the opposing skip as to whether or not the stone has come to rest in the Free Guard Zone. If the skips cannot agree, an official will be asked to make the determination by using the 6-foot (1.8-m) measuring stick. If the position of another stone hinders the use of the 6-foot measure, the official will reposition this stone, complete the measurement, and replace the stone in its original position.

5. In all other aspects the normal rules of play shall apply.

GENERAL STRATEGIES

The Three-Rock Rule

The Approach

The FGZ allows the opportunity for offense at all times during the game, but you must be careful not to get caught and overwhelmed by the idea. There are many games played today by big-name curlers that are over in a matter of four ends. Skips who gamble with the FGZ when they or their players aren't in touch with the conditions are prime to get blown out. The Free Guard Zone can be played in a defensive manner. A skip concerned about the abilities of his or her lead is smart to avoid getting drawn into playing the FGZ aggressively on every end.

There are some basic questions skips need to answer going into each end, whether or not they have last rock.

1. Are you at a point in the game where you feel it is essential for you to score?

2. Are you at a point in the game where you feel your team might be able to outplay the opponent (particularly at the lead position) on fine, delicate come-around shots?

3. Is using the defensive approach the best ploy at this time? The Skins Game format demands different parameters, and so does the FGZ. Therefore, you must explore new approaches to the existing concepts.

With Last Rock

One of three outcomes in each end is considered acceptable, depending on the circumstances. They are:

- Count two or more.

- Blank the end (no count).

- Surrender a steal of one to the opposition.

The first two options make sense; the third will require a little more explanation. The idea of counting two or more is obvious. There comes an interesting point, however, when a skip with last rock sometimes sizes up the situation, realizes two or more points are unlikely, and reverts to a blank-end strategy. Giving up a steal used to be bad news before the FGZ because good peeling teams could go on indefinitely wiping out front stones. Not any more. The FGZ guarantees at least one guard in front of the house at the start of each end, and offers teams a realistic chance of scoring at least two points with last rock. It now becomes far more acceptable to risk going for two, knowing it could backfire and the opponent steal one.

The opponent, under the Three-Rock Rule, will probably do one of two things with the first rock of the end if he or she doesn't have the hammer: Place the stone in front of the rings on the center line, about 4 feet (1.2 m) in front of the rings (Fig. 6.1, Position No. 1), or draw into the front of the 4-foot circle near the center line (Fig. 6.1, Position No. 2). Your next move will depend on the score and on the stage of the game you're at. Say your opponent goes for option No.1. You, as skip, might consider the following:

1. If the score is close and you feel confident of the ice conditions, you could attempt to bury the next stone around the guard into the 4-foot circle

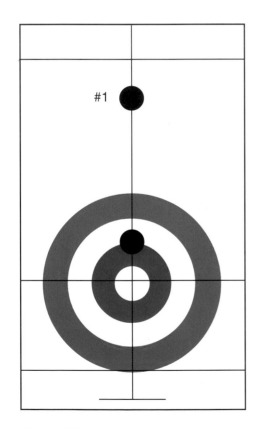

Figure 6.1

(Fig. 6.2). If this shot is well played, you have the makings of a possible two, or bigger, end. However, if things fall apart, your opponent could be positioned to steal one or more points.

2. If you are down points, you will probably consider one of two moves. First, you could go around the front guard immediately and attempt to bury in the 4-foot circle. Another option is to place a second guard on either side of the existing guard to provide maximum cover for a possible count of two or more (Fig. 6.3). It is highly unlikely your opponent, up by two or more points, would intentionally put a stone in this position. If he or she did, it is a sign that the strategy is to play around the guard, if possible, with the next shot.

3. If you are up two or more points, your opponent will likely hit first stone out front, toward the center line. Now it's decision time. You can either play offensive and draw around the guard with your next stone, or play defensively. Today's competitive teams will play a defensive shot known as the "tick." It's played exactly how it sounds. The "tick" is a quiet weight takeout in which the guard is "ticked" or rubbed away from the center line and close to the dividing boards (Fig. 6.4). Moved too far, however, and the guard is placed back to its original position.

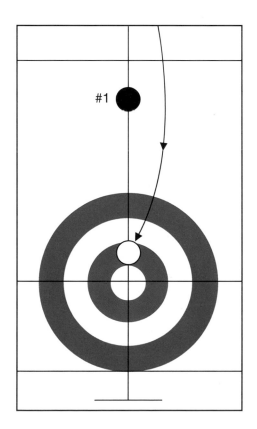

Figure 6.2

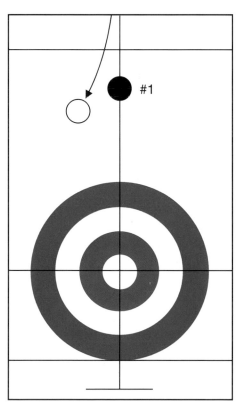

Figure 6.3

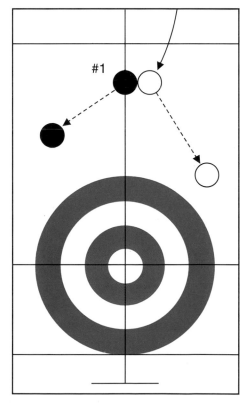

Figure 6.4

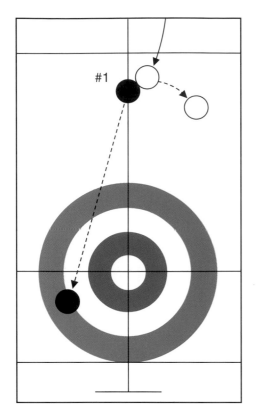

Figure 6.5

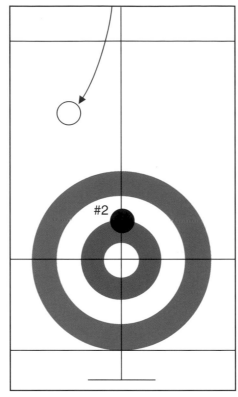

Figure 6.6

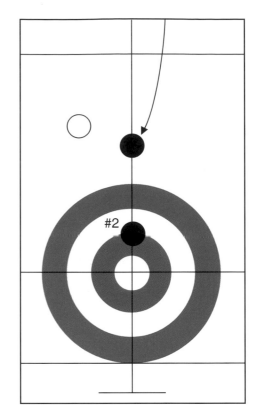

Figure 6.7

Figure 6.8

Another option, and one that is seldom played, is to throw a stone with precise weight and push the guard into the back of the 12-foot circle, meanwhile rolling the shooter away from the center line (Fig. 6.5). This is a positive shot because, no matter what your opponent does with the third stone of the end, you will have an open stone in the circles to remove from play. The guard out front also belongs to your team, setting up a possible raise if needed later in the end.

Say your opponent plays option No. 2. You might consider the following:

1. When the score is close and you're ready to pounce with two or more points, there are a couple of logical moves. First, establish a corner guard to provide the best opportunity to bury (Fig. 6.6). It's a risky move because there is a good chance your opponent will come back with a center guard, and then the game is on (Fig. 6.7). A little less risky but still an intelligent play would be a draw shot in front of the stone in the 4-foot circle (Fig. 6.8).

2. If you are down points, there is little question you should establish a corner guard. The only other option would be to consider a guard in front of the stone in the 4-foot circle. This would force the game to be on because your opponent will have to consider throwing a second guard on top of the one you placed to further protect his or her stone in the 4-foot.

This could lead to all kinds of interesting possibilities, including a steal by your opponent.

3. If you are up points, it is unlikely the opponent will play a stone into the rings. If that happens, you should remove it immediately.

Without Last Rock

Once more, one of three possible outcomes is acceptable. They are:

- Force your opponent to take one.

- Steal one or more.

- Allow your opponent to score no more than two.

Before the FGZ, skips hoped the opponent would take a single, give up one, or blank the end. Given a choice, skips would probably choose to give up a single and regain control of last rock. Skips could also afford to wait several ends for the opposition to make a mistake, and then pounce by scoring two key points. But the FGZ takes the sting out of giving up two points. It is no longer critical because, in the next end, with last rock, you have an excellent chance to score two or more points and be right back in the game.

With the three-rock FGZ, you have three options with your first stone of the end when the opponent has the hammer: Throw the stone about 4 feet (1.8 m) in front of the circles toward the center line (Fig. 6.9); draw the 4-foot circle, stopping in front of the tee line (Fig. 6.10); or throw the stone through the rings. Here's the strategy behind each shot:

1. If you place your initial stone of the end out front near the center line, you are making an offensive statement and should be prepared to back it up with some touchy, come-around shots before the end is over. If, however, the stone is thrown close to the center line but tight to the house, and your opponent draws around it, that leaves the option of the raise-takeout with your next shot.

2. A stone drawn to the 4-foot circle is definitely a less aggressive approach. You will have to see what your opponent does next. Your opponent could get aggressive and throw the next stone out front, to either side of center line, leaving you with a decision (Fig. 6.11). An offensive decision would be to throw a center guard on your stone in the circles, fairly tight to the rings, making the come-around tap-back difficult or impossible. A conservative decision would be to throw the next stone to the open side of the rings and split the house, leaving everything in the open (Fig. 6.12). This will put more pressure on your opponent, who is now facing two stones in the rings. If desperate, your opponent could throw up another guard or attempt to draw behind the existing corner out front (Fig. 6.13).

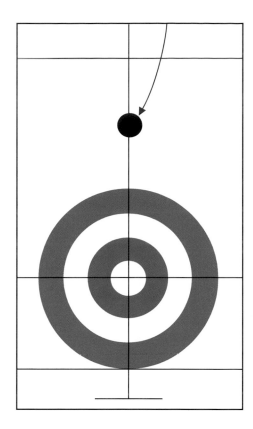

Figure 6.9

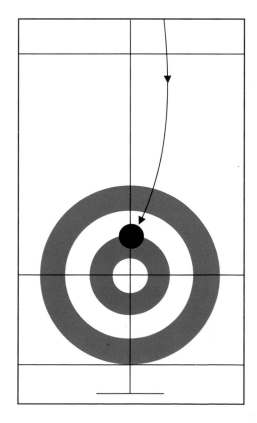

Figure 6.10

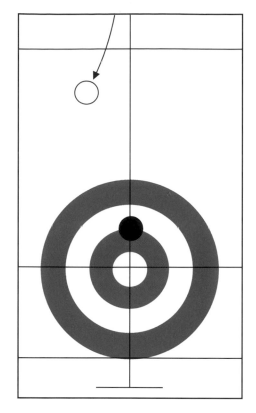

Figure 6.11

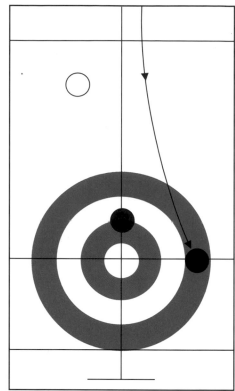

Figure 6.12

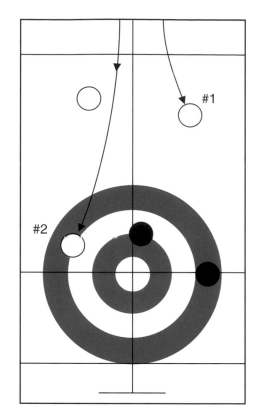

Figure 6.13

3. There are a couple of occasions in a game to consider throwing a stone through the rings. If you are up three or more points and do not want to provide your opponent with any sort of an offensive opportunity, a throw-through makes sense. Also, if you unsure whether your opponent plans to play aggressively, a throw-through will force the issue.

The Four-Rock Rule

The Approach

The three-rock FGZ and the four-rock FGZ may appear to be similar on the surface, but the approach to playing each one is different. The Three-Rock Rule, as noted previously, can be played with defense in mind. However, it is much more difficult to play defensively with the Four-Rock Rule.

Key Factors of the Four-Rock FGZ:

1. An attacking, offensive style of play.

2. Play limited to the center of the sheet.

3. Patience is the key. Skips must be prepared to wait for an end to unfold.

4. The start of each end is similar to play using the Three-Rock Rule.

Without Last Rock

If you do not have the hammer, there are three options with your first rock of the end: Place it out front toward the center line; draw into the 4-foot circle near the center of the house, in front of the tee; throw it through the rings. Here's the strategy behind each shot:

1. Guard Out Front This is probably the most common approach used with the Four-Rock Rule, but it should be used intelligently. If it is early in the game, or you have the lead, you may want to try something else. However, use it when: (a) the game has passed the early ends and you want to force the opponent's hand; (b) you are down in the game at any time; (c) you want to prove to your opponent early that your team is better at the delicate come-around game.

2. Rock in the 4-Foot Early in the game and during that "feeling-out" process, this is a smart play. Your opponent can't ignore a stone in the house if it is properly positioned—in front of the tee line and fully in the 4-foot. This should ensure play in the house for the first few rocks of the end and present no trouble for your team. Your opponent could counter with a corner guard, but that shouldn't lead to trouble either.

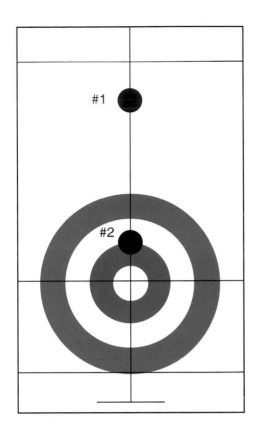

Figure 6.14

3. Throw-Through If you are holding a big lead at any time in the game, the throw-through makes sense. Your opponent wants rocks in play, and this eliminates one of them right off the top. No doubt your opponent will throw out a corner guard, so think about what you can live with. If you are prepared to give up two (assuming your opponent plays a perfect end), then also throw the second stone through. If you wish to apply some pressure, consider drawing around the opponent's guard.

With Last Rock

There are three choices to consider after the opposition has delivered the first of the end. In most cases, your opponent will place the rock out in front near the center line, draw it into the top of the 4-foot, or throw it through the rings (Fig. 6.14).

1. Guard Out Front If the stone is fairly tight to the circles, you have five possible options. Which one you play will depend on the score, ice conditions, the ability of your players, and the strength of the opposition. The options are:

a. Draw around the guard and bury in front of the tee line. This is an option that wouldn't normally be used in the Three-Rock Rule (Fig. 6.15). Still, it must be thought out. How good is your lead at making this shot? Is there enough curl in the ice to bury the stone? It must be buried perfectly— behind the guard and in front of the tee line—to be of any use.

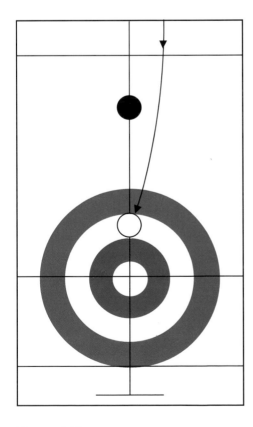

Figure 6.15

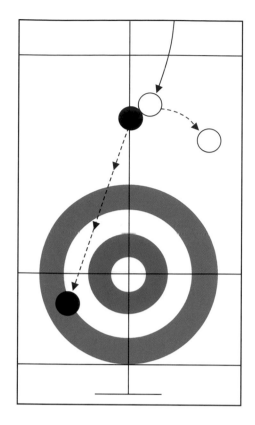

Figure 6.16

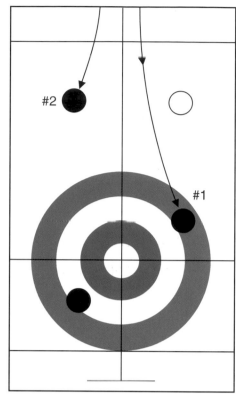

Figure 6.17

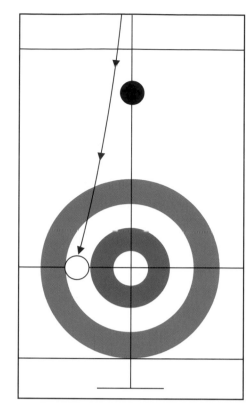

Figure 6.18

b. Push the opponent's guard to the back rings and roll the shooter slightly to the outside. This is the shot in the Four-Rock Rule that you might consider rather than playing the three-rock tick (Fig. 6.16). This shot allows you to play a hit with your next stone (on the stone in the house or the guard that remained out front as a result of the raise). Expect your opponent to draw around the guard or place another guard out front (Fig. 6.17). In any case, you are left with a hit of some sort and one less excuse for getting involved in a complicated come-around game.

c. Play the tick on the guard. It's a dangerous gamble because, if you miss, your opponent will probably place a second guard out front that you're not allowed to peel with the lead's last stone (this is the major difference between the Three-Rock and Four-Rock rules). There are certain times to try the tick, but not late in the game.

d. Draw to the 8-foot circle, away from the guard. Many curlers don't believe in using this option, but it will depend on the positioning of the rock and what you think your opponent will do next. To be effective, the stone can't be too far to the outside and must be at, or slightly back, of the tee line, and fully in the 8-foot (Fig. 6.18). If your opponent has nerve, he or she will ignore this shot and come around and bury behind the front stone. It's a gamble because if he or she slides behind the tee or sits in the open, you could play the takeout and quickly have the advantage. Ideally, you want the opposition to make a play on your stone. Even a well-played hit-and-roll behind the tee leaves you a shot. It is essential for your initial draw not to stop in front of the tee because the perfectly played hit-and-roll would end up behind the guard and in front of the tee line.

e. Throw the stone through the rings. This is not a smart option. Instead, attempt the tick. If missed, the result is the same as a throw-through.

2. Rock in the 4-Foot Circle If the first stone comes to rest at the top of the 4-foot, you have two options: Hit the rock and remove it, or freeze down to it (this might result in the stone being pushed back slightly behind the tee line). Unless you are desperate, don't consider the corner guard.

a. Remove the stone in the 4-foot circle. This is the safest approach, especially early in the game, during the "feeling out" process.

b. Freeze to the stone, or push it back behind the tee line. A freeze to the face of the stone is great, but pushing the opposition stone behind the tee line is just as good (Fig. 6.19). Either shot forces the opposition to make a play on your stone and, perhaps, jam it onto their own, meanwhile rolling out with the shooter.

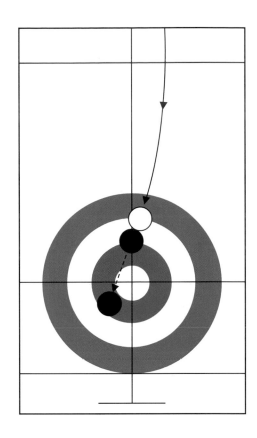

Figure 6.19

c. Throw up a corner guard. Many curlers use this option, but it is not advised (Fig. 6.20). Almost without exception, your opposition will counter with a guard out front, protecting his stone in the house. The Three-Rock Rule gives you the option of a run-through, or at least a peel of the front guard. This is not the case with the Four-Rock Rule. You could, with your next stone, play the tick or push the guard over, or into the rings. However, your opponent may quickly replace the guard.

d. Throw the rock through the rings. This is a likely play if your opponent has a big lead. Your best counter is a center, or corner guard. Your opponent will probably play the tick next, which is tougher to execute on a center guard than with a corner guard.

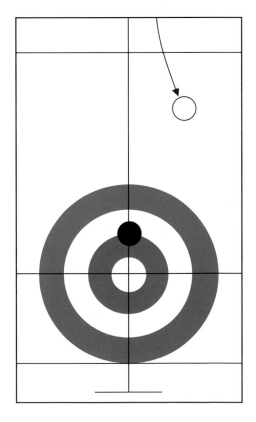

Figure 6.20

The Future

After reading this book and learning about the growth and development of curling around the world in the past decade, it's easy to conclude the future of the sport is bright and prosperous. And for many reasons it is. More countries than ever are playing the game, it has full-medal status at the Olympic Games, and television coverage and ratings of Canadian events are going through the roof. Pretty good stuff. Still, the sport has some major hurdles to overcome in the next decade, even in Canada.

Curling is huge in Canada, and an integral part of the history and sport culture of the country. Canadians love the game. Close to one million of them play it at 1,200 clubs across the country. Meanwhile, the national attention and television coverage curling gets ranks right up there with big attractions like hockey and figure skating. Curling's major championships, such as the Labatt Brier, Scott Tournament of Hearts, and the Ford Worlds, are smash hits, attracting record numbers of spectators and boffo television numbers.

Still, all is not well with the curling clubs in Canada. A number of clubs have closed their doors in the past decade, and many others are hanging on by their fingernails. It gets worse: nowhere is there evidence that curling's participation numbers are increasing. In fact, they are falling.

How can that be? Didn't we just say how popular the game is on television and the huge inroads it has made at the elite level?

Sadly, the facts are on the table. Curling's numbers are going down simply because curling clubs are not doing the job of recruiting new people. And the game has stagnated at the club level, where programs haven't changed much in fifty years.

If you were to take a sampling in any region, you would find three types of clubs: those that are doing very well, those doing so-so, and those struggling to keep the wolf from the door. The most successful clubs hustle to recruit new members, blend them into existing programs, and do whatever it takes to make them happy. They understand that the future is in young players, and have focused on their junior programs. The clubs treading water are usually resting on their laurels and bending to the whims of long-time members who resist change. They see no need to revamp or retool. Meanwhile, few juniors join up and there is little potential for growth. Clubs in the most trouble have simply paid little or no attention to bringing in new players.

Curling clubs have a challenge. They must get with the times and start bringing new blood into the sport. They can start by revamping many of their archaic programs. Clubs need to work at making the product serve the needs of the customer. If you don't know how to play the game and you aren't part of a team, it's very difficult to go into a club and become part of what's going on. Novice leagues and competitions are needed. Individuals, or pairs, who want to join clubs also need to be given greater consideration.

Curling clubs in Canada face other serious problems. The tax structure, for one, is crippling many clubs. It's ridiculous when you think that people play on soccer fields and hockey rinks in communities and pay virtually nothing for the privilege. Curling offers the same type of recreation facility to the public, yet clubs are taxed to the hilt by almost every municipality in the country, meanwhile paying hydro bills that are way out of sight. In many cases, assessments are so disproportionate and property taxes so high that clubs are closing their doors.

The curling community in Canada was stunned last year when a House of Commons subcommittee tabled a report recommending significant tax breaks for Canadian-based professional sports teams. It's ironic that the federal government suggests professional sport deserves funding while most municipal governments provide little or no assistance to the development of curling—one of the largest participation sports in the country.

The curling community needs to bond together and provide a unified front to pressure politicians at all levels. We know that about one million people in Canada curl, or about 1/30 of the population. If there's one thing all politicians understand, it's re-election. Curlers can make a pretty strong statement at the ballot box if politicians refuse to address the woes of the curling clubs.

Canada's top competitive curlers have a dream of a professional circuit that would resemble golf's PGA Tour. It's an interesting idea but has one serious flaw—it won't fly unless Americans are involved in a big way. It's this simple: Canada's 30-million population cannot produce the television revenue or the sponsorship dollars required to make it work.

The future of curling around the rest of the world is iffy. Certainly the key is in the vast market of the United States. Interest in curling in the United States today is relatively small, and the game is played primarily in states that hug the 49th parallel. The rest of the country, unfortunately, could care less about the sport, which is why television coverage is non-existent. That has to change in the next five to ten years. The Winter Olympic Games in 2002 at Salt Lake City is a great place to start. Curling will be a medal sport at Salt Lake City for the second time, and Americans will be among the teams participating. The time is ripe to tap into the huge U.S. television and sponsorships markets.

Somehow, curling has to be part of the network coverage of the Games. Curling blew a golden opportunity at the 1998 Olympic Games in Japan when it failed to get even one minute of air time on the major networks. It could happen again in Salt Lake City unless a major curling lobby can convince NBC that curling works on television.

Japan is another potential growth area. The game intrigued thousands of Japanese during the Nagano Olympics, and with a little more nurturing the game could take off. But don't bet on it happening. There are not nearly enough facilities in Japan, and not much chance they will be built because of the high price of property in the country.

Curling's past, not its future, is in Europe. The average European doesn't play because there are not enough facilities and it's expensive to play. Curling has done pretty well in Scotland, Sweden, and Switzerland, because all those countries actually have places to play. Still, sponsorship in these countries is small by Canadian standards, and television exposure limited.

Curling has some major problems to overcome in every region of the world. But if it can get the Americans interested in the game, starting with coverage of the Olympic Games on network TV, then the future will be a whole lot brighter.

Appendix

THE ASSOCIATIONS

Canadian Curling Association
2540 Lancaster Road
Ottawa, ON
K1B 4S5
(Tel) 613-748-5628
(Fax) 613-748-5713
Web site: www.curling.ca

United States Curling Association
1100 Center Point Drive
Box 866
Stevens Point, WI 54481
(Tel) 715-344-1199
(Fax) 715-344-2279
Web site: www.usacurl.org

The World Curling Federation
81 Great King Street
Edinburgh, Scotland
EH3 6RN
(Tel) 44 131 556 4884
(Fax) 44 131 556 9400

WCF MEMBER NATIONS

1. Canada
2. Scotland
3. United States
4. Sweden
5. Switzerland
6. Norway
7. Germany
8. France
9. Denmark
10. Italy
11. England
12. Netherlands
13. Wales
14. Austria
15. Finland
16. Luxembourg
17. Japan
18. Australia
19. Bulgaria
20. Hungary
21. Belgium
22. Czechoslovakia
23. Andora
24. Iceland
25. Liechtenstein
26. Mexico
27. New Zealand
28. Korea
29. Romania
30. Russia
31. U.S. Virgin Islands
32. Belarus
33. Chinese, Taipei
34. Brazil

Olympic Demonstration Sport

Women

1988—Canada: Linda Moore, Lindsay Sparkes, Debbie Jones-Walker, Penny Ryan

1992—Germany: Andrea Schopp, Stephanie Mayr, Monika Wagner, Sabine Huth

Men

1988—Norway: Eigil Ramsfjell, Sjur Loen, Morten Sogaard, Bo Bakke

1992—Switzerland: Urs Dick, Jurg Dick, Robert Hurlimann, Thomas Klay

Olympic Medal Sport

Women

1998—Canada: Sandra Schmirler, Jan Betker, Joan McCusker, Marcia Gudereit

Men

1998—Switzerland: Patrick Hurlimann, Patrik Loertscher, Daniel Muller, Diego Perren

CANADIAN CURLING HALL OF FAME AND MUSEUM OF CANADA INDUCTEES

Nominations to the Curling Hall of Fame are submitted on an annual basis to the Hall of Fame selection committee. The committee meets annually to review nominees, selecting those who meet the criteria in one of four categories: curler, builder, curler/builder, team.

Men

Aitken, Donald J.	1979	Curler
Allan, J.W.	1974	Builder (Inaugural provincial association president)
Anderson, Dr. A.F.	1976	Builder (CCA p-pres. 1941)
Angus, A.F.	1974	Builder (Inaugural provincial association president)
Anton, Ronald M.	1975	Curler (Two-time Brier winner)
Argue, Horace F.	1974	Builder (Inaugural provincial association president
Armstrong, James E.	1976	Builder (CCA p-pres. 1947)
Armstrong, Dr. James P.	1990	Curler
Auger, Henri	1974	Builder (Inaugural provincial association president)
Avery, Francis (Frank)	1974	Builder
Balderston, Norman	1988	Builder
Baldwin, Matthew M.	1973	Curler (Three-time Brier-winning skip)
Belcourt, Timothy	1991	Curler/team
Bennett, Hon. Gordon L.	1976	Builder (CCA p-pres. 1967)
Boreham, H. Bruce	1975	Builder
Bourne, Earl E.G.	1976	Builder (CCA p-pres. 1962)
Boyd, Earl	1974	Builder (Inaugural provincial association president)
Boyd, H.E.	1974	Builder (Inaugural provincial association president)
Boyd, Ralph S.	1989	Builder (CCA p-pres. 1986)

Boyd, W. Cecil	1976	Builder (CCA p-pres. 1955)
Buxton, Noel R.	1987	Builder
Cameron, Douglas A.	1974	Curler (Seven-time Brier competitor)
Cameron, George J.	1973	Builder
Cameron, R.W. (Bert)	1975	Builder
Campbell, Hon. Brig. Colin A.	1973	Builder (CCA p-pres. 1948)
Campbell, Glen M.	1974	Curler (Six-time Brier competitor)
Campbell, Gordon	1975	Builder
Campbell, Dr. Maurice	1976	Builder (CCA p-pres. 1971)
Campbell, Hon. Thane A.	1974	Builder (CCA p-pres. 1942)
Campbell, W. Garnet	1974	Curler (Ten-time Brier competitor)
Carstairs, Kent	1991	Curler/team
Carter, Harry P.	1976	Builder (CCA p-pres. 1969)
Congalton, James	1975	Curler (Two-time Brier winner)
Cowan, Walter B.	1976	Builder (CCA p-pres. 1960)
Cream, Robert C.	1976	Curler
Culliton, Hon. Edward M. (Ted)	1974	Builder
Currie, D. William	1976	Builder (CCA p-pres. 1974)
Deacon, Keith	1974	Builder (Inaugural provincial association president)
Delmage, Al R.	1991	Curler/builder
Dillon, George V.	1974	Curler (Eight-time Brier competitor)
Dillon, Robert F.	1974	Curler (Seven-time Brier competitor)
Donahoe, James E.	1973	Curler/team (First Brier winner)
Donahoe, Hon. Sen. Richard A.	1976	Builder (CCA p-pres.)
Duguid, Donald G.	1974	Curler/team (Three-time Brier winner)
Dutton, John	1976	Builder (CCA p-pres. 1957)
England, J. Irl	1976	Builder (CCA p-pres. 1973)
Ferbey, Randy	1993	Curler/team
	1995	Curler (Two-time Brier winner)
Ferguson, John	1992	Curler/team
Fisher, Thomas R.	1986	Builder (CCA p-pres. 1982)
Folk, Richard D. (Rick)	1985	Curler/team
Fortier, H.C. (Rene)	1974	Builder
Fox, Gordon	1994	Builder
Gatchell, William	1995	Builder
Geary, Reginald H.	1979	Builder
Gervais, Hector J.	1975	Curler (Two-time Brier winner)
Good, William, Sr.	1992	Builder
Gooder, Edwin	1982	Builder
Gow, Hon. Peter	1974	Builder (Inaugural provincial association president)
Gowanlock, Albert (Ab)	1975	Curler (Two-time Brier winner)
Grant, William A.	1975	Curler (Two-time Brier winner)
Gray, Maj. Thomas	1977	Curler/team (The Red Jackets)
Gunn, John	1987	Curler/Mixed team

Gunnlaugson, Lloyd H.	1989	Curler
Gurowka, Joseph A.	1989	Builder (CCA p-pres. 1989)
	1993	Curler/builder
Hackner, Allan A.	1988	Curler/team
	1992	Curler (Two-time Brier winner)
Haig, Hon. Sen. John T.	1973	Builder
Hall, Perry G.	1974	Curler (Six-time Brier competitor)
Harper, Geo. M. (Scotty)	1974	Builder
Harris, Bill	1999	Builder
Harrison, Neal	1991	Curler
Harstone, Ross. G.L.	1974	Builder
Haynes, J. Gordon	1975	Curler (Two-time Brier winner)
Heartwell, Robert J.	1990	Builder
Hobbs, Walter	1977	Builder
Houston, Neil	1992	Curler/team
Howard, Glenn	1991	Curler/team
Howard, Russell	1991	Curler/team
Hudson, Gordon M.	1974	Curler (Two-time Brier winner, CCA p-pres. 1950)
Hunter, Roderick G.M.	1974	Curler (Two-time Brier winner)
Jackson, Niven M.	1976	Builder (CCA p-pres. 1951)
Kawaja, John	1991	Curler
Kennedy, Bruce	1988	Curler/team
Keys, John E.	1979	Curler
Kingsmith, Raymond A.	1986	Builder (CCA p-pres. 1984)
	1994	Builder
Lamb, Arthur N.	1979	Builder
Lang, Richard P. (Rick)	1988	Curler/team
	1992	Curler (Three-time Brier winner)
Langlois, Allan D.	1975	Curler (Two-time Brier winner)
Leaman, William E.	1977	Builder (CCA p-pres. 1976)
Lewis, Donald E.	1989	Builder
Lobel, Arthur L.	1979	Curler
Low, William	1974	Builder (Inaugural provincial association president)
Lucas, Frederick J.	1974	Builder
Lukowich, Edward	1992	Curler/team
Lumsden, William E.	1976	Builder (CCA p-pres. 1968)
Lyall, Lt. Col. Peter D.L.	1973	Builder
Mabey, Harold L., Sr.	1975	Builder
Macdonald, Dr. Wendell L.	1975	Builder
	1977	Curler
MacGowan, Alan N.	1976	Builder (CCA p-pres. 1961)
MacInnes, J. Alfred	1973	Curler/team (First Brier winner)
MacKay, Elbridge P.	1976	Builder (CCA p-pres. 1939)
MacKay, William J.	1975	Builder

MacKenzie, Donald	1993	Curler/team
MacKinnon, Daniel D.	1974	Builder (Inaugural provincial association president)
MacLeod, Donald R.	1990	Builder (CCA p-pres. 1990)
Macneill, Murray	1973	Curler/team (First Brier winner)
Magrath, W.J.	1974	Builder (Inaugural provincial association president)
Malcolm, John S.	1974	Builder
Manahan, Clifford R.	1975	Curler (Two-time Brier winner)
Mather, J.B.	1974	Builder (Inaugural provincial association president)
Maxwell, Douglas D.	1996	Builder
Mazinke, Harvey G.	1989	Builder (CCA p-pres. 1988)
McArthur, J.B.	1974	Builder (Inaugural provincial association president)
McEwen, Cameron	1977	Builder
McGibney, Doug (Buzz)	1978	Curler
McGrath, Larry	1987	Curler/mixed team
McGraw, Thomas	1977	Curler/team (The Red Jackets)
McNeice, Burd S.	1979	Builder
McWilliams, Andrew	1975	Curler (Two-time Brier winner)
Millham, Herbert C.	1986	Builder (CCA p-pres. 1978)
	1992	Builder
Mills, Ronald A.	1985	Curler/team
Mittom, Lorne	1994	Executive Honor Role (CCA p-pres. 1995)
Moss, John	1993	Curler/builder
Murchison, Clifford A.L.	1981	Builder
Muzika, Jerry J.	1988	Builder (CCA p-pres. 1987)
Ness, R. Bruce	1975	Builder
Nicol, Robert B.	1988	Curler/team
Norgan, George W. (Bill)	1976	Builder (CCA p-pres. 1942-1946)
Northcott, Ronald C.	1973	Curler (Three-time Brier-winning skip)
O'Brien, Frank	1979	Builder
Olson, L.F. (Bud)	1976	Builder (CCA p-pres. 1975)
Olson, Stanley	1992	Executive Honor Role (CCA p-pres. 1993)
Opaleychuk, Dr. Clyde R.	1986	Builder (CCA p-pres. 1985)
Parish, A. William	1974	Builder
Parkhill, Albert J.	1976	Builder (CCA p-pres. 1969)
Pattee, James G. (Ted)	1975	Builder (CCA p-pres. 1963)
Perroud, Patrick	1995	Curler (Two-time Brier winner)
Perry, Capt. Charles	1977	Curler/team (The Red Jackets)
Pettapiece, James K.	1974	Curler (Two-time Brier winner)
Pickering, Robert H.	1974	Curler
Piercey, William F.	1975	Builder
Pollard, Ernest	1975	Curler (Two-time Brier winner)
Rankine, H. Fielding	1976	Builder (CCA p-pres. 1953)
Rennie, Thomas H.	1973	Builder
Richardson, Arnold W.	1973	Curler/team (Four-time Brier winner)

Richardson, Carleton S.	1974	Builder
Richardson, Ernest M.	1973	Curler/team (Four-time Brier winner)
Richardson, Garnet S. (Sam)	1973	Curler/team (Four-time Brier winner)
Richardson, Wesley H.	1973	Curler/team (Three-time Brier winner)
Rockwell, Norman P.	1978	Builder
Rothschild, Samuel	1975	Builder (CCA p-pres. 1958)
Ryan, Patrick	1993	Curler/team
	1994	Curler (Three-time Brier winner)
Samson, Olivier	1978	Builder
Sargent, Frank F.	1974	Builder (Inaugural provincial association president, CCA p-pres. 1966)
Savage, A. Paul	1988	Curler
Sinclair, John A.	1974	Builder (Inaugural provincial association president)
Singbusch, Ronald	1975	Curler (Two-time Brier winner)
Skinner, F. Arthur	1976	Builder (CCA p-pres. 1965)
Smart, James	1974	Builder (Inaugural provincial association president)
Smith, David C.	1978	Builder (CCA p-pres. 1977)
Smith, Sir Donald	1973	Builder
Smith, Emmett M.	1974	Builder (Inaugural provincial association president, CCA p-pres. 1954)
Sparkes, Bernard L.	1974	Curler (Three-time Brier winner)
Squarebriggs, John D.	1978	Curler
Steeves, Dr. Edward	1991	Executive Honor Roll (CCA p-pres. 1991)
Stent, Frank M.	1986	Builder (CCA p-pres., provincial association president)
Stewart, David Macdonald	1974	Builder
Stewart, T. Howard	1973	Builder
Stewart, Walter. M	1973	Builder
Stone, Reginald E.	1974	Curler
Stone, Roy H.	1974	Curler
Storey, Frederick L.	1973	Curler (Three-time Brier winner)
Syme, Brent	1992	Curler/team
Tarlton, A. Ross	1982	Builder
Tetley, Ian	1999	Curler
Thibodeau, Nicholas J.	1975	Builder
Thonger, Ted	1999	Builder
Thompson, G. Clifton	1986	Builder (CCA p-pres. 1979)
Thompson, T. Gordon	1976	Builder (CCA p-pres. 1972)
Tomalty, Gerry	1999	Curler/builder
Topping, Richard T.	1976	Builder (CCA p-pres. 1964)
Torey, Clifford L.	1973	Curler/team (First Brier winner)
Tracy, William R.	1982	Curler
Travers, Thomas	1974	Builder (Inaugural provincial association president)
Trites, Evan A.	1985	Builder
Turnbull, Raymond	1993	Curler/builder

Tyre, James	1974	Builder (Inaugural provincial association president)
Ursel, James W.	1979	Curler
Walchuk, Donald J.	1993	Curler/team
	1995	Curler (Two-time Brier winner)
Walker, David	1977	Curler/team (The Red Jackets)
Walsh, William J.	1975	Curler (Two-time Brier winner)
Walters, Cyril F.	1986	Builder (CCA p-pres. 1983)
Watson, Grant G.	1974	Curler (Three-time Brier winner)
Watson, J. Kenneth	1973	Curler (Three-time Brier-winning skip)
Watt, Cecil M.	1986	Builder (CCA p-pres. 1981)
Webb, Horace P.	1975	Builder (CCA p-pres. 1970)
Weldon, Kenneth B.	1982	Curler
Welsh, James Oddie	1983	Curler
Werenich, Edward	1988	Curler
Weyman, Hugh E. (Jim)	1974	Buildcr
Willis, Errick F.	1974	Builder
Wilson, Archibald E.	1976	Builder (CCA p-pres. 1959)
Wilson, James R.	1985	Curler/team
Wilson, Thomas R.	1985	Curler/team
Wood, Bryan D.	1974	Curler/team (Two-time Brier winner)
Wood, D.J. Howard, Sr.	1974	Curler (Three-time Brier winner)

Women

Adams, Diane	1994	Curler/team
Ball, Caroline	1985	Curler/builder
	1986	Builder (CLCA p-pres. 1981)
Bartlett, Sylvia Ann (Sue-Ann)	1987	Curler
Barraclough, Marilyn	1990	Builder (CLCA p-pres. 1989)
Bergasse, Morag	1986	Builder
Betker, Jan	1999	Curler/team
Bodogh, Marilyn	1999	Curler
Bray, Shirley	1991	Curler/builder
Calles, Ada	1976	Curler
Clift, Kathleen (Kay)	1986	Builder (CLCA p-pres. 1971)
Cooke, Margret E.	1986	Builder
Corby-Moore, Edith	1976	Builder (CLCA p-pres. 1978)
Cragg, Pauline M.	1986	Builder (CLCA p-pres. 1963)
Crosby, Elsie	1988	Builder (CLCA p-pres. 1987)
Delisle, Noreen	1986	Builder (CLCA p-pres. 1983)
DeWare, Mabel Sen.	1986	Curler/builder
	1986	Builder (CLCA p-pres. 1975)
Dillon, Catherine	1995	Curler/builder
Dockendroff, Marion	1986	Builder (Inaugural provincial association president, CLCA p-pres. 1973)

Dwyer, Patricia	1992	Curler
Elliott, Jessie	1980	Builder
Farnham, Emily B.	1993	Curler/builder
Fedoruk, Hon. Sylvia	1986	Builder (CLCA p-pres. 1972)
Ford, Atina	1999	Curler/team
Foster, Barbara	1991	Builder (CLCA p-pres. 1990)
Hansen, Ina	1976	Curler
Gudereit, Marcia	1999	Curler/team
Hebb, Ann	1976	Builder (Inaugural provincial association president, CLCA p-pres. 1965)
Hill, Darlene	1987	Curler/mixed team
Houston, Heather	1994	Curler/team
Jamieson, Hazel I.	1982	Curler
Johnson, Clara	1976	Builder (Inaugural provincial association president)
Jones, Colleen P.	1989	Curler
Jones-Walker, Debbie	1991	Curler
Kaufman, June	1989	Curler/senior team
Kennedy, Tracy	1994	Curler/team
Kerr, Eva	1986	Builder (CLCA p-pres. 1982)
Kerr, F. Marjorie	1986	Builder (CLCA p-pres. 1974)
Knox, Sharon	1986	Builder (CLCA p-pres. 1984)
Konkin, Irene	1987	Builder
Krahn, Evelyn	1989	Curler/senior team
	1994	Executive Honor Roll (CCA-p-pres. 1992)
Lang, Lorraine	1993	Curler
	1994	Curler/team
LaRocque, Penny	1989	Curler
Light, Ina	1990	Curler/builder
Little, Shirley	1989	Curler/senior team
Linkletter, Betty	1976	Builder (Inaugural provincial association president)
Lytle, Velma M.	1976	Builder (Inaugural provincial association president)
Macdonald, Elizabeth	1990	Curler/builder
MacLean, Aileen	1987	Builder (CLCA p-pres.1986)
MacMurray, Mary	1976	Builder (Inaugural provincial association) president)
MacRae, Dorothy (Dot)	1989	Builder (CLCA p-pres. 1988)
Manley, Hadie	1990	Curler
Martin, Flora	1979	Curler
McCusker, Joan	1999	Curler/team
McKee, Joyce	1975	Curler (Five-time Canadian champion)
	1976	Curler/team
McLuckie, Lura	1978	Builder
	1986	Builder (CLCA p-pres. 1968)
Merry, Janet E.	1983	Builder
	1986	Builder (CLCA p-pres. 1977)

Messum, Edna	1993	Curler
Mews, Olive	1976	Builder (Inaugural provincial association president)
Moore, Linda	1991	Curler
Morash, Shirley	1996	Executive Honor Roll (CCA President 1995-96)
More, Christine M.	1988	Curler
Morrison, Lenore (Lee)	1976	Curler/team
Myers, Joyce	1989	Curler/builder
New, Dorothy D.	1986	Builder (CLCA p-pres. 1980)
Nicholson, Mary-Anne	1992	Executive Honor Roll (CCA p-pres. 1992)
Orser, Anne	1999	Curler
Pezer, Dr. Vera	1976	Curler (Three-time Canadian champion)
	1976	Curler/team
Piers, Peggy	1984	Curler/builder
Pike, Violet	1983	Curler
Porter, Muriel	1976	Builder (Inaugural provincial association president)
Proulx, Rita C.	1976	Builder (Inaugural provincial association president)
	1986	Builder (CLCA p-pres. 1979)
	1987	Curler/builder
Reid, Pat	1999	Executive Honor Roll (CCA p-pres. 1997)
Roper, Barbara	1976	Builder (Inaugural provincial association president)
Rowan, Sheila	1976	Curler/team
Rowlands, Marion	1976	Builder (Inaugural provincial association president)
Roy, Adeline M.R.	1977	Builder
Schmirler, Sandra	1999	Curler/team
Segsworth, Mabel Dalton	1976	Builder (Inaugural provincial association president)
Sinclair, Marjorie H.	1976	Builder (CLCA p-pres. 1964)
Snowdon, Jean	1982	Builder (CLCA p-pres. 1970)
Sparkes, Lindsay E.	1988	Curler
Thompson, Dorothy	1978	Curler
Tipping, Edith	1986	Builder (CLCA p-pres. 1985)
Tobin, Lee	1979	Curler
Turner, Thora	1980	Builder
Vandekerckhove (Vande), Patti	1989	Curler
Wallace, Jo	1986	Builder (CLCA p-pres. 1969)
Watson, Islay (Ila)	1976	Builder (Inaugural provincial association president)
Watt, Hazel	1986	Builder (CLCA p-pres. 1961)
Whalley, Joan	1981	Builder
	1986	Builder (CLCA p-pres. 1976)
Whitehead, Elma-Mae	1989	Builder (Inaugural provincial association president)
Widdifield, Twyla	1989	Curler/senior team
Wooley, Emily	1975	Curler
Wood, Nora	1979	Builder
Youngson, Muriel	1986	Builder (CLCA p-pres.)

Glossary

BACK LINE The line across the ice at the back of the house. Stones over this line are removed from play.

BACK RING The portion of the 8-foot and 12-foot rings behind the tee line.

BITER A rock that barely touches the outer edge of the 12-foot circle.

BLANK END A scoreless end with no rocks in the rings.

BLANKING AN END Deliberately creating a blank end for the purpose of retaining last-rock advantage in the next end.

BONSPIEL A curling competition comprising a number of different events.

BRUSH A device used to sweep the ice in the path of a moving stone.

BUMPER, OR BACK-BOARD WEIGHT A stone thrown with sufficient momentum to reach the back board.

BUTTON The circle at the center of the house.

CHIP To hit only a portion of a stone.

COUNTER Any stone in the rings or touching the rings that is a potential point.

CURL The amount a rock bends while traveling down the sheet of ice.

DOUBLE TAKEOUT A takeout shot that removes two opponent stones at one time.

DRAW WEIGHT The momentum required for a stone to reach the house or circles at the distant end.

END A portion of a curling game that is completed when each team has thrown eight stones and the score has been decided.

FOUL A stone that is released from the curler's hand after it has crossed the nearer hog line.

FREE GUARD ZONE (FGZ) RULE See Chapter 4, Strategy.

FREEZE A shot on which an attempt is made to have a moving stone come to the face of a stationary stone without moving the stationary stone.

FRONT RING The portion of the 12-foot circle that is in front of the tee line.

FUDGED When a rock is slowed down unexpectedly in a certain portion of ice that is usually slower as a result of the pebble being worn down.

GUARD A stone that is placed in a position so that it may protect another stone.

HACKS The footholds at each end of the ice from which the stone is delivered.

HACK WEIGHT A stone delivered with enough momentum for it to travel to the hack at the distant end.

HAMMER The last stone of an end.

HEAVY A rock delivered with a greater force than necessary.

HIT A takeout. Removal of a stone from the playing area by hitting it with another stone.

HOG LINE A line 33 feet (10 m) from the hack at each end of the ice.

HOGGED STONE A stone that does not reach the far hog line. It must be removed from play.

HOUSE The four rings (circles or head) toward which the rock is delivered.

IN-TURN The rotation applied to the handle of a stone that causes it to rotate in a clockwise direction and curl for a right-handed curler.

JACK A marker that is established as a target.

JAM When a front rock is raised onto a back stone when that was not the result desired.

JUNK The style of play that has many stones in play.

LEAD The first curler on a team to deliver a pair of stones for his team in each end.

LIGHT A stone delivered with less than the weight required to successfully complete the desired shot.

NARROW A rock delivered inside the intended path or target, which is the skip's broom at the distant end.

OUT-TURN The rotation imparted to a stone that starts it turning in a counter-clockwise direction for a right-hander and a clockwise direction for a left-hander.

PEBBLE A fine spray of water applied to a sheet of curling ice before commencing play.

PEEL A takeout shot that removes a stone from play and the delivered stone also rolls out of play. A peeled rock is usually a guard in front of the circles.

PICK When a rock catches a brush hair or a foreign object on the ice that changes the rock's direction.

PORT An opening between two stones that is large enough to allow passage of another stone.

RAISE When one rock is bumped ahead by another.

ROLL The movement of a curling rock after it has struck a stationary rock in play.

RUN A straight spot in the ice that is usually caused by a dip or hollow that will not allow the rock an opportunity to curl out of it. Like a "rut" in the ice.

RUNNER A takeout shot that travels very fast.

SHOT ROCK At any time during an end, the stone which is closest to the button.

SECOND The curler who delivers the second pair of stones for his or her team in each end.

SHEET The ice upon which curling is played.

SKIP The fourth or last member of the curling team who generally delivers the last pair of rocks and also directs the strategy of the game.

STRAIGHT HANDLE, OR DEAD HANDLE A rock that doesn't have either an in-turn or an out-turn rotation.

SWEEPING The action of moving a broom or brush back and forth in the path of a moving stone.

SWINGY ICE Ice on which the "draw" of a stone is greater than normal.

TAKEOUT Removal of a stone from the playing area by hitting it with another stone.

TEE LINE The line that passes through the center of the house and runs at a right angle to the center line.

THIRD, VICE-SKIP, OR MATE The third player on a team to throw two stones in each end.

TICK An attempt to move over a stone in the FGZ with the second to fourth stone of an end (the fourth rock only with four-rock FGZ) without taking the stone out of play.

TURNED IN A stone which, at release, is directed toward the target or target area and not directly at the skip's broom.

WEIGHT The momentum imparted to a curling stone in delivery.

WICK To hit only a small portion of a stone.

WIDE The delivery of a rock outside the target, and consequently off the line of delivery.

Index